The
Arendell Parrott Academy
Cookbook

Making Time

Published by
Arendell Parrott Academy
Kinston, North Carolina
1998

This cookbook, developed by the Mothers' Committee, is a collection of time-conscious recipes from parents, students, alumnae and friends of Arendell Parrott Academy. All are family favorites. We do not claim that any of them are original. Proceeds from the sale of this cookbook will be used to further the academic excellence of our students.

Additional copies of *Making Time* may be obtained by using the order forms in the back of this book or by writing to:

The Arendell Parrott Academy Cookbook

Making Time

P. O. Box 1297
Kinston, North Carolina 28503
252-522-4222

First Printing 1998 5000 copies

Printed in the USA by
WIMMER
The Wimmer Companies
Memphis
1-800-548-2537

Table of Contents

(Please note that upon the recommendation of the Wimmer Co., brand names have not been used in recipe ingredient lists.)

3

Introduction

In the rush of our everyday activities, we often don't take the time to slow down, relax and enjoy the simpler things in life. Often, time to spend in the kitchen just isn't available. If you take a moment to browse through this book, we think you'll find recipes that will let you find the time. Pull up a chair, sip a cup of tea and enjoy Making Time.

Paul Lichstein

Cookbook Committee

Chairman
Susan King

Assistant-Chairman
Julie Hoell

Recipe and Steering Committee

Nancy Deichmann	Linda Peacock
Dedee Dunn	Sylvia Poole
Bonnie Everette	Janet Ricciarelli
Jill Gravely	Kim Stokes
Holly Hill	Tucker Talley
Stephanie Hill	Julie Tipton
Lisa Hines	Betty Lou Trimboli
Maryanne Klein	Marty Vainright
Susan Luper	Elizabeth Wooten
Marti Mostellar	Michelle Zeph
Laura O'Brien	

Special Events and Publicity

Faith Greenwood, Co-Chairman	Lisa Marshall
Alice Tolson, Co-Chairman	Julie Tipton

*The Arendell Parrott Academy Mothers' Committee extends its heartfelt grati-
tude to Susan King and her family for the countless hours of dedication they
have contributed to making this cookbook a reality.*

5

Illustrations

Daniel Drummond

Winslow Goins

Judy Johnson, APA Staff

Andy King

Paul Lichstein

Jim Ostrowski

Dinah Sylivant

Cover Art

Designed and produced by Judy Johnson

A very special thanks to Judy Johnson for her generosity and talent.

A sincere thank you to all of our contributors, without whose generosity this publication would not have been possible.

We are particularly grateful to Betty Johnsey and Linda Page, Co-Chairmen of Frantic Elegance, for their leadership and legacy.

Beverages
&
Appetizers

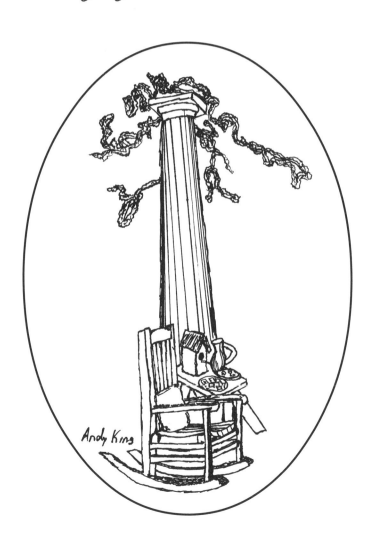

Andy King

After Practice Beverage

1	egg	½	teaspoon vanilla
1	tablespoon sugar	1	cup boiling milk

Place egg, sugar and vanilla in blender. Turn on and add milk. When well blended, pour into saucepan and heat over medium heat five minutes. Keep in thermos.

R.C. Wingerter, class of 91
J. Wingerter, class of 93

Fruit Freeze

2	cups water	1	can frozen orange juice (mix)
2	cups sugar	1	quart pineapple juice (sweetened
5	mashed bananas		or unsweetened)
1	can frozen lemonade (mix and pour over bananas)		

Boil two cups water and two cups sugar until sugar dissolves. Mix all ingredients in a large container. Pour into two shallow pans and freeze. Cut into squares, place in large zip-top plastic bag and return to freezer. Use as needed. To use place four squares in a blender and add one liter of ginger ale or lemon-lime drink. Blend to a slushy texture.

Diane With

Shrub

3	ripe bananas, mashed		juice of 2 lemons
1	cup sugar	2	cups orange juice
1	(15 ounce) can crushed pineapple	2	cups lemon-lime drink or ginger ale

Combine all ingredients except lemon-lime drink. Freeze. Allow to thaw to a slushy consistency before serving. Add lemon-lime drink or ginger ale.

Yield: 12 servings

Jenette Low

Iced Citrus Sun Tea

2½ cups orange juice
4   tea bags
4   cups water
1   lime, sliced

1   lemon, sliced
¼   cup simple syrup
1   orange, sliced

Fill ice tray with orange juice and freeze. Combine tea bags and water and steep four hours at room temperature. Stir in syrup and fruit slices. Serve over orange juice cubes.

Simple Syrup:

1½ cups sugar

1¼ cups water

Boil until dissolved. Cool and chill.

Dina Trimboli Whitley, class of 80

Malted Cocoa Mix

1   package (25.6 ounce) nondairy milk powder
6   cups miniature marshmallows
1   container (16 ounces) instant cocoa mix for milk

1   jar (13 ounces) malted milk powder
1   cup sifted confectioners sugar
1   jar (6 ounces) nondairy powdered creamer
½   teaspoon salt

In a large bowl, combine dry milk, marshmallows, cocoa mix, malted milk powder, confectioners sugar, creamer and salt. Stir until well blended. Store in an airtight container in a cool place. To serve pour six ounces hot water over ⅓ cup cocoa mix. Stir until blended. Yields 20 cups mix (10 gifts)

Carla Lancaster

Peach Champagne

2	large cans sliced peaches	2	large bottles champagne, chilled
1	fifth peach brandy	1	two liter bottle club soda, chilled

Drain most of the syrup from the peaches. Soak peaches in brandy overnight. When ready to serve, pour peaches and brandy into punch bowl. Add cold champagne and club soda.

Faith Greenwood

That Punch

1	(6 ounce) can frozen orange juice concentrate, thawed	2	cups bourbon (optional)
1	(6 ounce) can frozen lemonade concentrate	1	(2 liter) bottle lemon-lime carbonated beverage
½	cup lemon juice	1	(10 ounce) bottle club soda

Combine first four ingredients and chill. Stir in lemon-lime and club soda. Pour over crushed ice.

Yield: 3 quarts

Marie Dailey, class of 76

Thick Strawberry Whip

1	pint fresh strawberries, cleaned and hulled (reserve several for garnish) or 2 cups frozen strawberries	1	can sweetened condensed milk
		2	cups crushed ice

Combine all ingredients in blender in order listed. Blend until smooth. Garnish with strawberries if desired. Mixture stays thick and creamy in refrigerator.

Yield: 4 cups

Erin Harrison

Bacon-Cheddar Cheese Ball

2   (8 ounce) packages cream
     cheese, softened
½   pound sharp cheddar cheese,
     grated
½   cup chopped green onion

6   slices bacon, cooked and
     crumbled
3   tablespoons diced pimento
3   tablespoons minced parsley

Combine all ingredients, blending well. Form into a ball. Cover with plastic wrap and refrigerate overnight. Serve with crackers.

Linda Haven

Bacon Quiche Biscuit Cups

nonstick spray
8   ounces cream cheese
2   tablespoons milk
2   eggs
½   cup shredded cheddar cheese

½   teaspoon dried minced onion
5   slices bacon, crisply cooked and
     crumbled
1   (12 ounce) can refrigerated
     flaky biscuits

Spray ten muffin cups. In medium bowl beat cream cheese, milk and eggs on low speed until smooth. Stir in cheese and onion. Set aside. Separate dough into ten biscuits. Place one biscuit in each cup. Firmly press in bottom and up sides forming ¼ inch rim. Place half of bacon in bottom of dough-lined cups. Spoon 1-2 tablespoons of cheese mixture over bacon. Top with remaining bacon. Bake at 375 for 21-26 minutes or until filling is set and edges of biscuits are golden brown. Remove and serve warm.

Yield: 10 servings

Linda Haven

Ham and Cheese Crisps

1	(17 ounce) package frozen puff pastry, two sheets	½	cup grated Swiss cheese
		6	ounces thinly sliced ham
2	tablespoons honey	1	egg, beaten
2-4	tablespoons Dijon mustard	2	teaspoons water

Thaw pastry twenty minutes. Line baking sheet with parchment paper or plain brown paper. On lightly floured surface, unroll pastry sheets. Spread mustard and cheese; top with ham. Starting at long edge, roll tightly jelly roll fashion. Chill one hour. With sharp knife, cut pastry roll into ½ inch slices. Arrange two inches apart on baking sheets. Cover and freeze up to one month. When ready to bake, brush with egg and water. Bake at 400 for 15-18 minutes.

Yield: 24 servings

Ham and Cheese Delights

2½	tablespoons prepared mustard	1	teaspoon Worcestershire sauce
1½	sticks butter or margarine, softened	2	packages party rolls
3	tablespoons poppy seed	1	pound thinly sliced ham
1	small onion	⅓	pound sliced Swiss cheese

Combine mustard, butter, poppy seed, onion and Worcestershire. Remove rolls from foil pans. Cut through the middle of rolls, separating top from bottom. Spread the blended ingredients on the inside of each of the rolls. Layer ham and cheese on the bottom half. Place top layer of rolls on stacked ham and cheese. Cut into individual rolls. Place back in original foil pans. Bake at 375 for 10 minutes. The rolls may be replaced in pans and plastic bags for freezing. Thaw 1 hour.

Eugenia Briley

Ham and Cheese Appetizers

2	cups biscuit baking mix	½	cup sour cream
¾	cup finely chopped smoked ham	2	tablespoons parsley
1	cup shredded cheddar cheese	½	teaspoon garlic salt
½	cup finely chopped onion	⅔	cup milk
½	cup grated Parmesan cheese	1	egg

Combine all ingredients and mix well. Spread into greased 9x13 inch baking pan. Bake at 350 for 25-30 minutes or until golden brown. Cut into 36 equal rectangles.

Yield: 36 servings

Linda Haven

Sweet and Sour Hot Dogs

1	(6 ounce) jar mustard	2	packages hot dogs
1	(10 ounce) jar red currant jelly		

Cut hot dogs into bite-sized pieces. Mix hot dogs, mustard and jelly in medium sauce pan. Simmer over low heat for approximately 20 minutes. This recipe won 1st place in a cooking contest sponsored by The Evening Telegram in 1977.

Elizabeth Hood

Sausage Dip

1	pound bulk sausage (hot or mild)	1	can diced tomatoes with green chilies
1	(8 ounce) package cream cheese		tortilla chips

Brown sausage, drain and crumble. Add cream cheese and tomatoes and chilies. Heat and stir until cream cheese is melted and all ingredients are mixed well. Serve in a chafing dish to keep warm. Serve with tortilla chips.

Yield: 2½ cups

Stephanie Hill

Crab Muffins

1	pound crabmeat	3	tablespoons mayonnaise
2	jars sharp, processed cheese spread	¼	teaspoon garlic powder
1	stick butter or margarine	1	teaspoon seasoned salt
		12	English muffins, split

Combine all ingredients, except muffins. Mix well. Spread on muffins. Quarter each muffin and bake on cookie sheet 10-15 minutes at 400. Muffins freeze well. Quarter and freeze prior to baking. Place frozen muffins in oven and bake at 400 until bubbly.

Yield: 12 servings

Faith Greenwood

Easy Crab Dip

1	pound imitation crabmeat	3	scallions, chopped
8	ounces cream cheese, softened	8	ounces shredded cheddar cheese

Mix first three ingredients and place in greased baking dish. Top with cheddar cheese. Bake at 350 for 20 minutes. Serve with crackers.

Carole Cameron

Hot Crab Dip

1	(7 ounce) can crabmeat	½	tablespoon Worcestershire sauce
4	ounces cream cheese, softened	1	freshly ground whole white pepper
1	tablespoon brand named horseradish mustard	2	tablespoons freshly grated Parmesan cheese
1	tablespoon lemon juice		

In small oven proof baking dish, mix together all ingredients except Parmesan cheese. Sprinkle with Parmesan cheese. Bake at 375 for 25 minutes or until hot and bubbly.

Erin Harrison

Oysters Rockefeller

4	tablespoons unsalted butter	¼	teaspoon salt
¼	cup dried bread crumbs		pinch ground black pepper
¼	cup sliced green onion		pinch cayenne pepper
¼	cup celery, chopped	12	fresh oysters on ½ shells
1	tablespoon chopped tarragon leaves		

Preheat broiler with rack 3-4 inches from heat. In food processor puree: butter, bread crumbs, onions, celery, tarragon, salt and peppers until smooth. Butter each oyster and broil until golden and crisp (2-3 minutes). Serve immediately.

Eugenia Briley

Marinated Shrimp

1	tablespoon sugar	1	teaspoon hot sauce
	salt and pepper to taste	1	green pepper, chopped
2	tablespoons dry mustard	1	medium onion, chopped
1	cup vinegar	1	clove garlic, minced
1	cup catsup	3	bay leaves
½	cup vegetable oil	3	pounds shrimp, cleaned and cooked
1	teaspoon steak sauce		

Mix sugar, salt, pepper and dry mustard with vinegar. Stir until smooth. Add remaining ingredients, except shrimp, and blend well. Pour over shrimp. Cover and chill at least 24 hours. Keeps for two weeks in refrigerator. Serve drained or in liquid.

Yield: 15 20 servings

Martha Flowers

Shrimp Toast

1½ pounds raw shrimp (about 1
　pound dressed)
½　medium onion, finely chopped
1¼ teaspoons garlic salt
1　tablespoon light soy sauce
1　teaspoon sugar

1　egg
2-3 tablespoons cornstarch
1　pound very thinly sliced white
　bread
oil

Chop ingredients, except bread until practically a paste. (5-10 minutes) Add seasonings, stirring well after each ingredient. Cut bread slices into four triangles and spread paste on each section. Heat 1 inch oil in pan. Bring oil to hot, then let it cool to medium heat. Cook on medium heat until golden.

Ella Rodgman

New Orleans Shrimp Pâté

2　(8 ounce) packages cream
　cheese, softened
2　tablespoons steak sauce
2　tablespoons hot sauce
2　pods garlic, minced
1　medium bottle cocktail sauce
1　pound mozzarella cheese, grated

6-8 green onions, chopped
1　green pepper, chopped
1　tomato, chopped, seeded and
　drained
1　pound cooked shrimp, crabmeat
　or ½ of each

Blend cream cheese, steak sauce, hot sauce and garlic. Spread in bottom of 9x13 inch or two 8 inch square containers. Top with cocktail sauce. Add shrimp, crab or combination. Sprinkle with grated cheese, onion, green pepper and tomato. Make a day ahead and this will keep for several days. Decorate with parsley or whole shrimp. Serve with crackers.

Yield: 12 servings

Lisa Williams Merriam, class of 78

Shrimp Spread

8	ounces cooked shrimp, cut into large chunks	4	tablespoons finely chopped onion
2	tablespoons lemon juice	2	cups finely chopped celery
1	cup mayonnaise	4	tablespoons catsup
2	tablespoons steak sauce	1½	pounds cream cheese, softened

Mix all ingredients. Allow to set 24 hours before serving. Serve with large wheat crackers.

Yield: will serve a crowd

Karen Williams

Chili Shrimp Dip

1	(10 ounce) can cream of shrimp soup	¼	cup finely chopped celery
1	(8 ounce) package cream cheese, softened	2	tablespoons finely chopped onion
			dash of steak sauce

Blend soup and cream cheese with electric mixer. Beat until smooth. Stir in remaining ingredients and chill at least four hours. Serve as dip with crackers or chips.

Erin Harrison

Shrimp Paste

1	pound shrimp, cleaned and boiled	½	stick margarine
			horseradish
1	(8 ounce) package cream cheese		hot sauce

Chop shrimp in blender. Blend with softened cream cheese and margarine. Add horseradish and hot sauce. Chill and serve with crackers.

Laura O'Brien

Shrimper's Wife Shrimp Mold

1	can tomato soup	2	pounds shrimp, cooked, peeled and chopped
3	(3½ ounce) packages cream cheese	½	cup chopped onion
½	package unflavored gelatin	½	cup chopped bell pepper
1	cup mayonnaise	½	cup chopped celery

Heat and blend cheese and soup until smooth. Remove from heat and add gelatin. Cool. Combine with other ingredients and pour into mold sprayed with nonstick cooking spray. Chill 24 hours.

Janet Buff

Down East Clam Dip

8	ounces cream cheese, softened		dash Worcestershire sauce
3	tablespoons mayonnaise	2	tablespoons grated onion
5	tablespoons sour cream	1	(6½ ounce) can clams, minced
¼	teaspoon lemon juice		dash of hot sauce (optional)

Combine all ingredients except clams, using some of the clam juice to obtain good dip consistency. Add drained clams. Season to taste.

Lisa Mumford Kluttz, class of 88

Hawaiian Cheesecake Dip

1	cup marshmallow cream	1	tablespoon orange juice
1	(8 ounce) package cream cheese, softened	1	teaspoon grated orange peel
½	cup crushed pineapple, well drained		dash ground ginger
2	tablespoons frozen coconut	1	(6 ounce) container frozen whipped topping

In food processor blend all ingredients except whipped topping. Fold in whipped topping. Serve in hollowed out pineapple or cantaloupe bowls with strawberries, honeydew and cantaloupe.

Linda Haven

Nancy's Tuna Salad Mold

3 (24 ounce) cans solid white
   tuna packed in water, drained
3 (8 ounce) packages cream
   cheese, softened
½ cup minced onions

½ cup minced celery
   seasoning salt
   lemon dill mix
   fresh ground pepper
   dill weed

Place tuna, cream cheese, onion, celery and seasonings in a large bowl and mix with electric mixer until smooth. Turn into 5½ cup mold sprayed with nonstick cooking spray. Refrigerate 24 hours. To unmold, place bottom of mold in hot water for about 30 seconds and tap out onto serving dish. Garnish with fresh parsley, paprika, sliced olives, pimento, almonds, capers and sweet or dill midget pickles. Serve with assorted crackers.

Nancy Ward

Lavosh

2 (8 ounce) packages cream
   cheese
1 package ranch dressing mix
2 green onions, chopped

4   12 inch flour tortillas
½-¾ cup chopped green pepper
½-¾ cup chopped celery
1   can sliced black olives, drained

Mix first three ingredients and spread equally on the tortillas. Sprinkle with remaining ingredients. Roll up in jelly roll fashion. Wrap each roll in plastic wrap and refrigerate for at least 8 hours. May be stored this way for up to two days. To serve, unwrap plastic wrap and slice rolls in 1 inch slices. Be creative; add such ingredients as chopped spinach, mushrooms, red pepper, crabmeat.

Yield: 4-8 servings

Lynda Blount

Apple Dip

8	ounces cream cheese	1	teaspoon vanilla
¾	cup brown sugar	1	teaspoon cinnamon
¼	cup butter or margarine		apples, sliced

In a saucepan, mix all ingredients, except apples, over medium heat, stirring constantly. Cool. Arrange apple slices on serving plate with dip in serving container in center. This has a taste similar to caramel apples.

Yield: 2 cups

Linda Haven

Fruit Dip

1 (8 ounce) package cream cheese, softened, may use low fat	cut up fruit (apples or strawberries)
1 jar marshmallow cream	1 tablespoon cherry juice (optional)

Combine cream cheese and marshmallow cream and place in serving dish. Serve with fruit.

Faith Greenwood

Cheese Wafers

8	ounces sharp cheddar cheese	½	teaspoon salt
½	cup butter	½	teaspoon paprika
½	cup margarine		cayenne pepper (optional)
2	cups plus 2 tablespoons all purpose flour		

Combine cheddar cheese and butter in large bowl. Beat until smooth. Add flour, salt and paprika. Stir well. Shape into ½ inch balls. Press in ¼ inch thickness. Place one inch apart on a lightly greased baking sheet. Bake at 450 for 4-7 minutes or until browned.

Judy Grant

Hot Pecan Spread

2	tablespoons milk	¼	cup finely chopped bell pepper
8	ounces cream cheese	⅛	teaspoon garlic powder
1	(2½ ounce) jar dried beef, shredded	½	cup sour cream
		2	tablespoons butter, melted
2	tablespoons onion flakes	½	cup pecans, chopped
¼	teaspoon pepper		melba rounds

Cream milk and cheese. Stir in beef, onion flakes, pepper, bell pepper and garlic powder. Fold in sour cream. Spread in a baking dish. Heat pecans in butter. Spread on top of cheese mixture. Bake at 350 for 30 minutes. Serve with melba rounds.

Yield: 6-8 servings

Linda McMullen

Baked Brie

1	round of Brie cheese (Camembert may be used)		cookie cutters
		1	box cracked pepper crackers
1	pastry sheet (thawed according to directions)		

Place Brie on pastry sheet. Pull up pastry sheet and cover side and part of bottom, being careful to make even folds around round edges of Brie. Turn over onto foil-lined baking pan so that Brie is completely covered with pastry. Decorate top with leaf shapes or other shapes cut from excess pastry. Bake 20-30 minutes or until golden brown. Serve with crackers.

Yield: 6-8 servings

Janet Carson Ricciarelli

Parmesan and Artichoke Rounds

1 (10 ounce) can refrigerator flaky biscuits or rolls	½ teaspoon onion juice
¾ cup mayonnaise	1 (4 ounce) can hearts of artichokes in water
¾ cup grated Parmesan cheese	paprika

Divide rolls into 36 sections and place on nonstick cookie sheet. Mix mayonnaise, cheese and onion. Spread on each dough section. Place a slice of artichoke heart on top of each section. Top with additional mayonnaise mixture. Sprinkle with paprika. Bake at 400 for 10-12 minutes.

Yield: 12-18 servings

Ruth Mollison

Pineapple Cheese Balls

2 (8 ounce) packages cream cheese, softened	¼ teaspoon salt
1 small can crushed pineapple, drained	2 cups chopped pecans
	crackers

Mix cheese, pineapple and salt. Roll into two large balls. Refrigerate until firm. Roll in pecans. Serve with crackers. Chopped green peppers, onions or pecans may be added to cheese and pineapple mixture for variety. Freezes well.

Faith Greenwood

Crunchy Crocodile Celery and Carrot Sticks

1 (8 ounce) package cream cheese, softened	3 tablespoons dried vegetable soup mix
4 ounces pasteurized process cheese sauce	32 (two inch long) celery sticks
	32 (two inch long) carrot sticks

In a medium bowl, combine cream cheese, cheese sauce and soup mix. Beat until well blended. Cover and chill. Serve as a dip with celery and carrot sticks.

Yield: 8 servings

Carla Lancaster

Mushroom Puffs

2	packages crescent dinner rolls	2	green onions, chopped
1	(8 ounce) package cream cheese	1	teaspoon seasoned salt
	at room temperature	1	large egg, beaten
1	(4 ounce) can chopped	2	tablespoons poppy seeds
	mushrooms, drained		

Lay out crescent roll dough and press perforations to seal. Mix cream cheese, mushrooms, onions and salt. Spread over dough. Roll up jelly roll fashion. Slice into 1 inch pieces. Brush with egg and sprinkle with poppy seeds. Bake at 375 for 10 minutes. Serve hot. This recipe can be prepared ahead up to the slicing point then frozen until time to bake. In fact, the mushroom roll is easier to slice if it is frozen.

Yield: 48 puffs

Stacy Brody

Stuffed Mushrooms

100	medium sized fresh mushrooms	1	cup mayonnaise
1	pound sausage, cooked, drained	1	cup dried bread crumbs
	and crumbled	1	teaspoon onion salt
¾	pound shredded mozzarella	1	teaspoon Worcestershire sauce
	cheese		

Remove stems from mushrooms and discard. Wash cap in cold water. Turn caps upside down to drain. Mix together all other ingredients. Mound mixture in mushroom caps. Place stuffed mushrooms in shallow baking pan. Bake at 350 for 10-15 minutes. Serve hot. May be frozen before baking. Thaw 20-30 minutes, then bake.

Yield: 30 servings

Leraine Collier

Tomato Tart

1	deep dish pie crust		olive oil
4	ounces goat cheese, softened		salt and pepper
1¼	pounds ripe tomatoes, sliced thin	1	teaspoon dried thyme
		1½	tablespoons pine nuts

Bake pie crust for 9-11 minutes. Cool crust. Spread with goat cheese. Top with tomatoes. Sprinkle with olive oil, salt, pepper, thyme and pine nuts. Cut into wedges to serve.

Yield: 6 servings

Dina Trimboli Whitley, class of 80

Gorilla Gorp

1	(5 ounce) package round cheese puffs	1	cup raisins
3	cups round sweetened fruit flavored cereal	3	cups small pretzel twists
		1	(6 ounce) package fish shaped cheese crackers
2	(1.7 ounce) cans potato sticks		

In a very large bowl, combine all ingredients. Store in an airtight container.

Yield: 18 cups

Carla Lancaster

Chili Munchies

1	pound sage flavored sausage, cooked and drained	6	eggs, beaten
1	pound sharp cheddar cheese, grated	4	ounces chopped green chilies
		½	teaspoon chili powder

Sprinkle sausage in greased 9x13 inch baking dish. Cover sausage with cheese. Mix eggs, chilies and chili powder. Pour over sausage and cheese. Bake at 350 for 30 minutes. Cool and cut into cubes to serve. May serve warm or cooled.

Martha Flowers

Veggie Bites

2	(8 ounce) packages refrigerated crescent rolls
1	egg beaten
2	(8 ounce) packages cream cheese
1	cup mayonnaise
1	envelope ranch style salad dressing mix

¾	cup shredded cheese
½	cup chopped tomatoes
½	cup chopped broccoli
½	cup chopped green peppers
½	cup chopped mushrooms

Unroll crescent rolls and place in an ungreased jelly roll pan, pinching the edges together to seal. Brush with egg. Bake at 375 for 11-13 minutes. Cool. Combine cream cheese, mayonnaise and salad dressing mix. Beat until well blended. Spread mixture over crust. Sprinkle with cheese and veggies. Chill two hours. Cut into bite-sized pieces.

Yield: 8 dozen

Betty Andrews

Party Mix

1	stick margarine, melted
½	cup oil
1½	tablespoons Worcestershire sauce
1⅓	teaspoons garlic salt
1⅓	teaspoons seasoned salt
1⅓	teaspoons hot pepper sauce
2	cups corn bran

2	cups rice square cereal
2	cups corn square cereal or honey graham cereal
2	cups honey graham donut shaped cereal
1	cup cheese tidbits
	pecans and/or pretzels

Combine margarine, oil, salts and hot pepper sauce. Combine remaining ingredients. Pour margarine mixture over and stir to mix. Bake at 250 for 2 hours, stirring every 30 minutes.

Yield: enough for a crowd

Elaine Clark Taylor

Game Day Dip

8 ounces cream cheese, softened	⅓ cup chopped green pepper
8 ounces sour cream	¼ teaspoon Worcestershire sauce
2 cups shredded cheddar cheese	paprika
½ cup chopped country ham	crackers or corn chips
⅓ cup chopped green onion	

Beat cream cheese at medium speed until smooth. Add sour cream. Stir in cheese, ham, onion, pepper and Worcestershire. Spoon into ovenproof dish. Bake at 350 for 30 minutes. Sprinkle with paprika. Serve with crackers or corn chips.

Penny Pelletier Manning, class of 84

My City Cousin's Pesto Mold

¼ cup pine nuts, roasted 10 minutes	¾ cup Parmesan cheese
	3 tablespoons butter
2 cloves garlic	2 (8 ounce) packages cream cheese
1 cup fresh spinach	1 pound unsalted butter
1 cup fresh basil	1 jar sun-dried tomatoes, drained
½ cup fresh parsley	bland crackers
½ teaspoon salt	leaf lettuce
½ cup olive oil	

In food processor combine pine nuts, garlic, spinach, basil, parsley and salt. Chop. Add olive oil, Parmesan cheese and 3 tablespoons butter. Combine cream cheese and 1 pound unsalted butter. Set aside. In a small mold create this layered appetizer by layering the two mixtures beginning and ending with the cream cheese. When completed there should be six layers of cream cheese and five layers of pesto. Refrigerate overnight. Unmold and top with a jar of sun-dried tomatoes. Serve with bland crackers on a bed of leaf lettuce.

Yield: 12-18 servings

Lynda Blount

Black Bean Salsa

1   (15 ounce) can black beans,
     rinsed
1   (8 ounce) can whole kernel
     corn, drained
3   plum tomatoes, chopped
1   bunch green onion, chopped
1   jalapeño pepper, finely chopped

1   teaspoon cumin
3-4 drops hot sauce
4-5 drops lemon juice
cilantro, chopped to taste
salt and pepper to taste
tortilla chips

Mix all ingredients, except chips, together in bowl. Serve with tortilla chips.

Sallie Edwards Mayeux, class of 88

Cream Cheese
and Guacamole Mexican Dip

1   (8 ounce) package cream cheese,
     softened
2   tablespoons mayonnaise
dash Worcestershire sauce
½   teaspoon garlic powder

1   (6 ounce) tin frozen guacamole
     or avocado dip, thawed
1   (8 ounce) jar picante sauce,
     medium
2   green onions, finely chopped
tortilla chips

Cream together cheese, mayonnaise, Worcestershire and garlic powder. Spread on rimmed plate. Cover and chill at least one hour. Just before serving frost cheese mixture with guacamole/avocado dip. Frost with layer of picante sauce. Sprinkle with green onions. Serve with tortilla chips.

Faith Greenwood

Mary Elizabeth's Mexican Dip

2	cans refried beans	1	large package grated extra sharp cheddar cheese
½	package dry taco seasoning		
1	large container sour cream		nacho chips
sliced hot peppers, optional			

Spread mixture of refried beans, taco seasoning and salsa (enough to wet beans) on bottom of 9x13 inch baking dish. Cover with sour cream. (May add sliced hot peppers to sour cream, if desired.) Top with cheese and bake at 350 until cheese melts. Serve with nacho chips.

Betty Robertson

Mexican Layer Dip

1	can refried beans	1	bunch scallions
1	cup sour cream	1	large tomato, diced
1	cup mayonnaise	2	cups shredded cheddar cheese
1	package taco seasoning mix		tortilla chips
2	small cans green chilies		

Grease shallow dish. Spread beans in bottom of dish. Combine sour cream, mayonnaise and taco seasoning mix. Spread over beans. Layer green chilies, scallions and diced tomatoes. Cover with cheese. Heat until cheese melts. Serve with tortilla chips. Can be made fat free.

Yield: 12 servings

Suzanne Moore, class of 82

Tex Mex

2	cans bean dip	chopped green onions, as desired
8	ounces sour cream	chopped tomatoes, as desired
2	tablespoons mayonnaise	shredded cheddar cheese, as desired
1	package taco seasoning	tortilla chips

Spread bean dip on a dip plate. Combine sour cream, mayonnaise and taco seasoning. Spread over beans. Top with green onions, tomatoes and cheese. Serve with tortilla chips.

Joan Braswell

Frijoles con Queso

2	(16 ounce) cans fat-free refried beans	1	cup sour cream
1	(4 ounce) can chopped green chilies	2	cups grated reduced fat cheddar cheese
½	teaspoon ground cumin	2	scallions, finely sliced
			tortilla chips

Combine beans, chilies and cumin in bowl. Spread mixture in the bottom of a two quart casserole. Top with sour cream, spreading it evenly from edge to edge. Sprinkle cheese evenly over the sour cream. Bake approximately 15 minutes or until cheese melts. Remove from oven and top with scallions. Serve hot with tortilla chips.

Yield: 10-12 servings

Linda Peacock

Mrs. Murphy's Mexican Medley

1	(32 ounce) can refried beans or regular beans mixed with one packet taco seasoning mix	1	bunch green onions, chopped
		2	cups shredded cheese, sharp cheddar or Monterey Jack
1	pint sour cream		alfalfa sprouts
1	(4 ounce) can chopped green chilies	2	medium tomatoes, chopped
			tortilla chips
1	(4 ounce) can chopped ripe olives		

Layer all ingredients in order listed on large serving platter. Serve with tortilla chips. Can be made night before adding chopped tomatoes when ready to serve.

Yield: 20-25 servings

Carole Cameron

Honey Chicken Wings

3	pounds chicken wings		2	tablespoons vegetable oil
salt and pepper			2	tablespoons catsup
1	cup honey		½	clove garlic, chopped
½	cup soy sauce			

Cut off and discard wing tips. Cut each wing into two parts and sprinkle with salt and pepper. Combine remaining ingredients and mix well. Place wings in shallow casserole. Pour sauce over and bake at 375 until chicken is well done and sauce is caramelized, about one hour.

Yield: 12-15 servings

Kay Gross

Soups

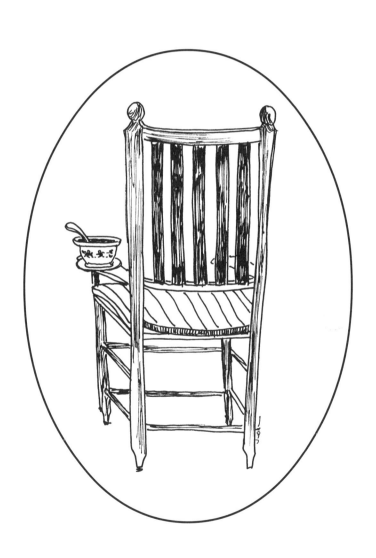

Beulah Knight's
Boarding House Brunswick Stew

3	pound pork roast	1	pound cabbage, shredded
5	pounds chicken	64	ounces catsup
2	pounds baby lima beans (dried may be used)	2	(16 ounce) cans whole kernel corn
2	pounds carrots, sliced	1-1½	gallons water
2	quarts tomatoes, diced	3	tablespoons salt and/or
2	pounds potatoes, diced		3 tablespoons sugar, optional

Preparation time: 4-5 hours or overnight if you choose to skim off fat from meats. Freezes great! Use large pot, 4 gallon minimum. Cook pork roast first 30 minutes in water. Add chicken(s) and boil until done, about 1-2 hours. Remove pork and chicken from broth. At this point you may cool the broth in the refrigerator overnight and skim off the fat the next day if you are following a low-fat diet. Debone and cut the meats into small pieces. Add the following ingredients to the boiling broth: carrots, onions, cabbage, tomatoes, potatoes and catsup. Cook at a slow boil for 30 minutes. Add chicken, pork and lima beans (presoaked, if dried). Cook slowly on low until tender. Add corn last and cook another 30 minutes on low. Stir frequently.

Yield: 3-4 gallons

P. S. Beulah! Please! Why so much?

Beulah Knight lived in Durham, NC with her husband, Haywood, three sons, Graham, Howard and Ralph, her father and stepmother, her three sisters (along with two husbands) and her brother at 420 Mangum Street. Needing additional income to feed this crowd, she began taking in boarders when Duke University brought in stone masons from Italy to construct the beautiful stone buildings on campus. In addition to boarding these foreign workers, she would take lunch to them in small glass bowls, wait for them to eat, then bring the dirty dishes back home.

Her husband worked at Liggett Meyers Tobacco Company where she would take his lunch. In addition she had a supply of shoe boxes she would stock with a meat, two vegetables (or one big bowl of Brunswick stew) and fresh lemonade and sell lunches to her husband's coworkers as well as those at American Tobacco Company

Beulah Knight's Boarding House Brunswick Stew continued

for 25 cents per meal (a real box lunch). Again she would return home with the shoe boxes, bowls and glasses to be cleaned and used again the next day.

She lived at this pace from the late 1920's until the late 1940's. There was a move at some point to a larger residence at 309 Holloway Street but never a change in lifestyle. Meal time at the Knights always involved such massive amounts of food.

Can the recipe be cut down? Probably. Have I ever done so? Never! It's just better to make it once a year (preferably in the fall), freeze it in meal-size containers and enjoy it for months to come. You see, Beulah Knight was my grandmother and she created this recipe. Enjoy!

Sylvia Knight Poole, dedicated to my memories of Beulah Knight, my grandmother and to my mother, Mavis Knight, who wrote down and saved this recipe for her children.

Corn Chowder

1	small yellow onion, minced	1	teaspoon salt
2	tablespoons butter	½	teaspoon celery salt
1	cup diced potatoes	1	cup milk
1	(10 ounce) package frozen kernel corn	1	cup light cream
		⅛	teaspoon white pepper
2	cups cold water or chicken broth		parsley, chives, or dill to garnish

In heavy saucepan stir fry onion in butter over medium heat until limp. Add potatoes, corn, water, salt and celery salt. Cover and simmer 10-15 minutes until potatoes are done. Sprinkle with parsley, chives or dill.

Yield: 4 servings

Marie Dailey, class of 76

Grandma Mabel's Brunswick Stew

1	medium hen, cooked in 1½ gallons water	1	quart tomatoes
1	pound ground beef	2	small cans tomato paste
2	cans butter beans	1	pound onions, chopped (optional)
2	cans garden peas	5	pounds potatoes, peeled
2	small bottles catsup	2	cans creamed corn
2	small bottles Worcestershire sauce		

Cook hen. Take meat off bones and put meat back into broth. Add ground beef and let boil for 45 minutes. Add butter beans, garden peas, catsup, Worcestershire sauce, tomatoes, tomato paste and onions. Cook potatoes, mash and stir into mixture. Add corn and season. Cook two hours over medium heat, stirring occasionally to prevent sticking.

Judy Grant

New England Chowder

3	(6 ounce) cans minced clams	1	cup chopped celery
¼	pound bacon	2	cups milk
2	cups water	1	cup half and half
4	cups diced potatoes	3	tablespoons all-purpose flour
½	cup chopped onion		salt and pepper to taste

Drain clams, reserving juice. In Dutch oven, fry bacon until crisp. Set bacon aside. Add clam juice, 2 cups water, potatoes, onions and celery. Cook covered 15-20 minutes. Add minced clams, 1¾ cup milk and half and half. Blend ¼ cup milk and flour; stir into chowder. Heat to boil, stirring occasionally. Salt and pepper to taste. Before serving, crumble bacon and stir into chowder. Serve with crackers.

Yield: 4-6 servings as dinner, 10-12 servings as appetizer

Betty Andrews

Easy Clam Chowder

2   (10 ounce) cans cream of potato
    soup
2   (6 ounce) cans minced clams
    with juice
1   (10¾ ounce) can cream of celery
    soup

1   cup milk
    pepper to taste
    parsley to taste
    onions or onion flakes to taste

Heat all ingredients together. Refrigerate leftovers.

Christian Cherry, class of 95

Creamed Barley Soup

¼   cup chopped shallots
¼   cup butter
1   cup pearl barley
5½ cups chicken stock

¼   teaspoon pepper
1   cup whipping cream
10 ounces frozen peas
1   cup grated Parmesan cheese

Cook shallots in butter until soft. Add barley; cook until golden. Add stock and pepper. Bring to a boil and simmer until barley is tender. Stir in cream and peas. Heat through. Serve with Parmesan.

Dina Trimboli Whitley, class of 80

Lentil Soup

2   (10¾ ounce) cans chicken or
    vegetable broth
1   onion, chopped

    olive oil
8   ounces dry lentils
3   carrots, grated

Sauté onion in very little olive oil in soup pot. Add remaining ingredients. Simmer 15 minutes over medium heat. Serve with crackers and Asparagus-Grapefruit Salad.

Joyce Witherington Mattux,
Sea Island Beach Club Spa, class of 77

35

Chicken Soup

4-6	chicken breasts with rib meat	1	(4 ounce) can sliced mushrooms
½	teaspoon garlic salt		(optional)
1	teaspoon salt	1-2	(10¾ ounce) cans chicken broth
¼-½	teaspoon pepper	1	(10 ounce) can cream of chicken
2	chicken bouillon cubes		soup
4	ribs celery, sliced	1	cup white rice, uncooked
3-4	carrots, sliced	1	teaspoon dried or 2 teaspoons
1	medium onion, chopped		chopped fresh parsley

Place chicken in 6-8 quart stock pot. Cover with water. Add garlic salt, salt and pepper. Cover and cook over medium-low heat 30 minutes. Remove chicken, cool, debone and cut into bite sized pieces. Skim excess fat from stock pot. Add canned broth, bouillon and vegetables. Cover and cook 15 minutes. Add cream of chicken soup, rice, parsley and mushrooms. Cover and lower heat. Cook 20 minutes. Add chicken. May need to add more broth to desired consistency.

Yield: approximately 1 gallon

Carole Cameron

Fall Festival Soup

1½	pounds ground beef	2	(10¾ ounce) cans tomato soup
	(or ½ ground beef and	2	cans water
	½ ground turkey)	1	tablespoon chili powder
1	cup chopped onion	1	small head cabbage, finely
1	quart tomatoes - crushed or		shredded
	diced		salt, pepper and sugar to taste
2	cups kidney beans		

Brown meat and onions; drain. Add all remaining ingredients and simmer 1½ hours. Season to taste.

Faith Greenwood

Chicken Curry Broccoli Soup

1	3-4 pound chicken	¾	cup uncooked rice
3	quarts chicken stock or broth	2	(16 ounce) cans tomatoes
2	bunches broccoli	1	tablespoon red pepper
1½	onions	2	tablespoons curry powder
2	stalks celery		dash of sage
1	carrot		salt and pepper to taste
2	tablespoons butter		

Cook chicken in stock or broth about one hour and a half over medium heat. When chicken is done, remove and let the stock simmer. Debone chicken. Tear into bite-sized pieces. De-stem broccoli, cutting and separating florets. Add chicken and broccoli to simmering stock. Mince onions, cut celery, shred or dice carrot. Sauté onions, celery and carrot in butter until translucent. Add vegetables to stock along with rice, tomatoes and spices. Simmer an additional 45 minutes.

Yield: 16 servings

Dedee Dunn

Meatball Soup

1	pound ground beef (round or chuck)	¾	cup pearl barley
2	tablespoons oil	2½	quarts water
1	large onion, or less, diced	½	cup parsley, chopped
3	ribs celery, chopped	2	cubes beef bouillon
1	(15 ounce) can quartered tomatoes	½	teaspoon oregano
			salt and pepper to taste
			garlic powder to taste

Make small meatballs of ground beef and brown in oil. Drain. Add remaining ingredients. Cook all together until barley is soft.

Yield: 10 servings

Sis Watts

Mushroom Bisque

1	pound mushrooms	1	cup cream
1	quart chicken broth	1	teaspoon salt
1	medium onion, chopped		pepper
7	tablespoons butter		hot pepper sauce
6	tablespoons flour	2	tablespoons sherry
3	cups milk		

Reserve and slice 6 mushroom caps. Chop remaining mushrooms very finely. Simmer, covered, in broth with onion for 30 minutes. Sauté reserved caps in 1 tablespoon butter. Reserve for garnish. Melt remaining butter. Add flour and stir until blended. Bring milk to boil and add to flour mixture. Stir until smooth. Add cream. Combine mushroom mixture with sauce and season to taste. Reheat and add sherry before serving. Garnish with sliced mushrooms.

Kay Gross

Toasty French Onion Soup

3-4	medium onions, chopped coarsely	⅛	teaspoon black pepper
¼	cup margarine or butter, melted	4	slices toasted French bread, or croutons to cover bottom of bowl
3	cans consommé soup	1	cup shredded mozzarella cheese
1	teaspoon Worcestershire sauce		

Sauté onions in butter in a Dutch oven over medium heat until onions are tender, stirring often. Add consommé soup, Worcestershire sauce and pepper. Bring to a boil then reduce heat. Cover and simmer 5 minutes. Ladle soup into individual ovenproof bowls over toasted bread or croutons. Top each dish with mozzarella cheese. Place under broiler until cheese is melted and browned. Serve immediately.

Yield: 4 servings

Faith Greenwood

Peach Soup

5   large fresh peaches, peeled and   1   quart water
    cut   1   ounce lemon juice
8   ounces brown sugar   1   ounce peach schnapps
1   ounce cinnamon

Place first four ingredients in a stainless steel pot. Cook until the
peaches start to mush. Allow to cool. Add lemon juice and schnapps.
Puree in blender. Chill before serving.

Yield: 8 servings

Joyce Witherington Mattux,
Sea Island Beach Club Spa, class of 77

Hearty Healthy Soup

Dried Ingredients:
1   (16 ounce) box split peas   1   (16 ounce) box barley
1   (16 ounce) box lentils   1   (2⅜ ounce) jar minced onion

Mix together and store in airtight container. Will use the rest for
another pot of soup.

2   pounds ground round   7   cups water
4   ribs celery, chopped   1   large can vegetable juice
4   carrots, sliced   2   (15 ounce) cans tomato sauce
1   cup shredded cabbage   salt and pepper to taste

Cook and drain beef. In separate pot cook carrots, celery and
cabbage in water until just tender. Add beef, juice, tomato sauce and
1½ cups of "dried ingredients" mixture. Cook on low heat about
2 hours. Season to taste.

*Hint: add ½ teaspoon black pepper and ¼ teaspoon red pepper in addition to
salt and pepper*

Kathy White

Spicy Potato Soup

1 pound ground beef, browned and drained	4 cups water
4 cups potatoes, peeled and cubed	2 teaspoons salt
1 small onion, chopped	1½ teaspoons pepper
3 (8 ounce) cans tomato sauce	½-1 teaspoon hot pepper sauce

In Dutch oven, combine beef, potatoes, onions and tomato sauce. Stir in water, salt, pepper and hot pepper sauce. Bring to a boil. Reduce heat and simmer for 1 hour or until the potatoes are tender and the soup has thickened.

Yield: 6-8 servings

Cathy Wellman

Nana's Homemade Vegetable Soup

1 pound ground beef	1 teaspoon minced garlic
1 soup bone with meat	1 small can tomato paste
water	½ cup barley
½ large head green cabbage, coarsely chopped	5 carrots, sliced
	1 small bag frozen white corn
2 large onions, coarsely chopped	1 small bag frozen small peas
1 green pepper, coarsely chopped	1 small bag frozen green beans
3 stalks celery, coarsely chopped	salt and pepper to taste

In very large soup pot, brown beef, crumbling. Add enough water to fill about ⅓ full. Add soup bone. Simmer while preparing other ingredients. In food processor, puree cabbage, onion, green pepper and celery by adding a small amount of water while processing. Add pureed mixture to soup pot. Add garlic, tomato paste and barley to soup pot. Simmer two hours, adding water if necessary. Add remaining ingredients and simmer an additional 1- 1½ hours. Remove soup bone and cool. Remove meat from bone and return meat and bone to soup. This freezes very well. Makes enough for a crowd. Always a favorite in the fall and winter. Cabbage is undetectable in the soup and leaves everyone asking, "What is in this soup that makes it taste so good?!"

Yield: enough for 20-30 servings

Elsie Fleckenstein, grandmother of Mark King

Quick and Easy Potato Soup

3   cans chicken broth (fat-free may   1   large onion, sliced
    be used)   1   stick margarine
6   large baking potatoes or small   1   can evaporated milk
    russet potatoes (use at least 8)   shredded cheese

Peel and cut potatoes in quarters and place in broth. Add onion and
boil for at least 20 minutes. Mash potatoes and add the margarine
and evaporated milk. Let simmer for 20-30 minutes. Serve hot with
shredded cheese on top.

Nancy Deichmann

Vegetable Soup

1   large can vegetable juice   1   (16 ounce) can of beans (kidney,
1   beef bouillon cube   black, butter beans, etc.)
1   (16 ounce) package frozen   Optional: 3 ribs celery, sliced,
    vegetables (carrots, corn, okra,   2 potatoes, diced, 1 onion,
    etc.)   chopped, 1 pound stew beef,
                                             ½ cup uncooked rice or pasta

Simmer for one hour. Enjoy. Leftovers can be frozen.

Joyce Witherington Mattux,
Sea Island Beach Club Spa, class of 77

Easy Vegetable Soup

2   cans mixed vegetables   1   teaspoon chopped parsley
1   can stewed tomatoes   1   teaspoon seasoning salt
2   cups vegetable juice   salt and pepper to taste

Combine all ingredients and bring to a boil. Turn heat down and let
simmer 15 minutes.

Yield: 6 servings

Hint: Low calorie

Shelia Hobgood

41

Tortellini Soup

1	teaspoon butter	1	(14½ ounce) can stewed
4	cloves garlic, minced		tomatoes
2	(14½ ounce) cans chicken broth	½	bunch spinach, washed and
1	(9 ounce) package cheese		stemmed
	tortellini	6	fresh basil leaves, chopped (or
½	cup grated Parmesan cheese		1 teaspoon dried basil leaves)
salt and pepper to taste		additional grated Parmesan cheese	

Melt butter in heavy, large saucepan over medium heat. Add garlic and sauté 2 minutes. Stir in remaining ingredients; bring to a boil; reduce heat. Garnish with additional Parmesan cheese and serve.

Yield: 4-6 servings

Stacy Brody

Nana's Steak Soup

2	pounds ground round, browned and drained	1	cup flour
		5	cups water
1	large package frozen mixed vegetables	1	large can chopped tomatoes
		1	teaspoon seasoning salt
½	cup chopped celery	½	teaspoon pepper
½	cup chopped carrots	2	tablespoons beef base
½	cup chopped onions	1	teaspoon browning and
1	cup chopped potatoes		flavoring liquid
½	cup margarine	1	teaspoon sugar

Prepare ground round. Set aside. Cook frozen vegetables, celery, carrots, onions and potatoes until tender. Set aside. Melt margarine and stir in flour to make a roux. Add water and cook until thick. Add meat, vegetables and remaining ingredients, except sugar. Simmer for ½ hour. Stir in sugar just before serving. The longer this soup sits, the better it gets. May be frozen.

Ellice DeBolt

Mom's Vegetable Soup

1½ pounds lean beef stew, cut into
    small pieces
2 (15 ounce) cans peeled tomatoes
1 center stalk celery
1 cup chopped celery
1 onion, whole
1 cup diced potato
1 cup garden peas
1 cup green beans
salt to taste
1-2 beef bouillon cubes

Cover beef with water and bring to a boil. Simmer. Add vegetables and salt. Add 1-2 beef bouillon cubes (to taste). Simmer until ready. When I was first married, Mom shared this wonderful recipe with me. As a new cook, she knew I would need explicit directions and so she began the recipe by saying put a large stock pot on the stove, wash the meat before cutting, etc. . .

Mary Ann Archie Swain, class of 74

Cream of Zucchini Soup

1 medium zucchini, thinly sliced
½ cup finely chopped onion
½ teaspoon minced garlic
1 tablespoon margarine or olive
    oil
1 chicken bouillon cube
1 cup boiling water
1 (10¾ ounce) can cream of
    potato soup
¾ cup milk
¼ cup white wine (optional)
1 tablespoon parsley
4 shakes (¼ teaspoon) hot sauce
salt and pepper to taste

In shallow skillet, heat margarine or olive oil on medium high. Add zucchini slices and sauté 1 minute. Add onion and garlic. Stir 1 minute. Turn heat to low, cover and cook 5 minutes or until zucchini is soft. Dissolve chicken bouillon in hot water. Spoon zucchini mixture into blender. Pour chicken broth over. Cover and puree about 45 seconds. Spoon in potato soup. Add milk and wine. Puree again until smooth. Pour into a pot. Add hot sauce and spices. Stir. If too thick add more milk or wine. Cover and heat on medium low about 20 minutes or until hot. Can be stored in refrigerator up to 3 days. Just add a little milk or water when reheating to achieve desired consistency.

Yield: 4 bowls or 6 cups

Vicki Hallberg

Archie's Gumbo

2 onions, diced	1 pound shrimp, peeled
1-2 cloves garlic, minced	1 cup rice, uncooked
olive oil	½ cup dry white wine
4 chicken breasts, cooked and broken into pieces	parsley
	filé, optional
1 package smoked sausage, sliced	1 large can tomato sauce

Sauté onions and garlic in olive oil. Add chicken, sausage, shrimp and rice. Add enough water to cover rice. Bring to a boil. Reduce to simmer and continue cooking, covered, 40-45 minutes, checking water level periodically. Add more water if necessary. Add wine, parsley, filé, and tomato sauce.

Yield: 6-8 servings

Cindy Archie

Crab Bisque

1 (10¼ ounce) can cream of mushroom soup	1 cup half and half
1 (10¼ ounce) can cream of asparagus soup	1 (6 ounce) can crabmeat, drained and flaked
2 cups milk	¼-⅓ cup dry white wine or sherry

Combine first 4 ingredients in saucepan. Heat thoroughly, stirring occasionally. Add crabmeat and wine. Heat thoroughly.

Yield: 6 cups

Kay Gross

Salads

Dinah Sylivant

Elegant Tossed Salad

1	head green or red leaf lettuce, washed and torn	1	teaspoon black pepper
8	roma tomatoes, diced	½	teaspoon lemon pepper
1	cucumber, diced	½	teaspoon thyme
1-2	slices onion, diced (optional)		crumbled bleu or feta cheese (optional)
⅓	cup prepared Italian dressing	8	medium-large rings of red onion (optional garnish)
1	tablespoon basil		
1	teaspoon salt		

Prepare lettuce for salad just before serving. Combine remaining ingredients (except for cheese and onion rings) 30 minutes - all day ahead. To serve, spoon generous amounts of seasoned vegetable mixture over prepared lettuce. Top with crumbled cheese and a red onion ring for color.

Yield: 4-5 servings

Jo Allen, class of 76

Seven Layered Salad

1	head lettuce	2	cups mayonnaise
1	cup shredded carrots	2	tablespoons sugar
1	large cucumber, sliced	2	cups shredded cheddar cheese
1	squash, sliced	1	package bacon, fried and crumbled
1	onion, sliced		
1	can small, young garden peas		

Place first six ingredients in salad dish in order listed. Combine mayonnaise and sugar. Spread over salad, covering completely. Refrigerate overnight. Just before serving, top with cheese and bacon.

Yield: 12 servings

Cindy Murphrey

46

Overnight Salad

1 head lettuce	1 pint frozen peas, cooked and cooled
3 ribs celery, chopped	
3 spring onions, chopped	Parmesan cheese
½ pound bacon, cooked and crumbled	shredded carrots

Layer ingredients in order listed. Cover with salad dressing and refrigerate 24 hours.

Yield: 8 servings

Louise Mauck

Romaine Salad

Salad ingredients:

2 heads romaine lettuce, washed and dried	1 purple onion, sliced
1 cup sliced mushrooms	6 slices bacon, cooked and crumbled

Dressing ingredients:

4 ounces bleu cheese, crumbled	½ cup white or red wine vinegar
1 tablespoon minced garlic	½ cup sugar
1 teaspoon salt	1 cup vegetable oil

Break lettuce into pieces and add mushrooms, onion and bacon in a large bowl. In separate bowl, mix all dressing ingredients until well blended. Just before serving add to salad and toss well.

Yield: 8-10 servings

Faith Greenwood

Crouton Salad

1 cup mayonnaise (regular, light or fat-free)
1 tablespoon lemon juice
2 tablespoons Parmesan cheese, finely shredded
1 clove garlic, crushed
1 tablespoon butter
1 cup croutons (cubed, day-old French bread)
2 heads lettuce (any type - leaf does well)

Make dressing of mayonnaise, juice, cheese and garlic. Chill. In saucepan toss croutons in butter over low heat until golden brown. Drain. Place torn lettuce in bowl. Add dressing and croutons. Toss, sprinkle with additional cheese.

Yield: 8 servings

Diane With

Frozen Cranberry Salad

2 tablespoons sugar
2 tablespoons mayonnaise
1 (8 ounce) package cream cheese
1 small container frozen whipped topping
1 can cranberry sauce with berries
1 small can crushed pineapple with juice
1 cup chopped nuts

Blend sugar and mayonnaise. Add cream cheese. Fold in whipped topping. Add remaining ingredients. Pour in muffin cups. Freeze. Take out 30 minutes prior to serving.

Yield: 20 servings

Cindy Beaman

Sour Cream Fruit Salad

1 large can fruit cocktail
4 cups miniature marshmallows
1 (8 ounce) container sour cream
1 cup flaked coconut

Mix all ingredients together and chill overnight.

Yield: 10-15 servings

Cindy Beaman

Apple Salad

2	tablespoons margarine, softened	4	apples, peeled and diced
¼	cup flour	1	container nondairy whipped topping
¾	cup sugar		chopped nuts
1	large can crushed pineapple in syrup, undrained		cherries

In a double boiler, combine margarine, flour, sugar and pineapple. Cook until thick. Cool and add apples. Spread in an oblong dish. Top with nondairy whipped topping, nuts and cherries.

Yield: 4-6 servings

Gloria Smith

Asparagus-Grapefruit Salad

	lettuce leaves	1	can asparagus spears
1	jar grapefruit sections		honey Dijon salad dressing

On lettuce leaf, place 3-5 asparagus spears and 3-6 grapefruit sections. Top with one tablespoon dressing.

Yield: 2-4 servings

Joyce Witherington Mattux,
Sea Island Beach Club Spa, class of 77

Frozen Fruit Salad

1	small can crushed pineapple with juice	¾	cup sugar
		1	teaspoon salt
1	can cherries, drained	2	tablespoons fresh lemon juice
1	(16 ounce) container sour cream	1	medium banana, mashed
		½	cup chopped pecans

Mix all ingredients and pour into small molds. Freeze.

Yield: 18 servings

Nancy Bower

Sallie's Fruit Salad

3   granny smith apples, peeled and diced
1   small bunch red seedless grapes, halved
1½ cups small marshmallows

1   (11 ounce) can mandarin oranges, drained
½-1 cup chopped walnuts
1   (8 ounce) container vanilla yogurt
zest of 1 lime

Combine all ingredients in a large bowl.

Yield: 4-6 servings

Sallie Edwards Mayeux, class of 88

Yum-Yum Salad

1   (20 ounce) can crushed pineapple with juice
¾   cup sugar
1   large box orange jello
2   cups cold water

1   cup grated cheese
1   large container frozen whipped topping
¾   cup chopped nuts

Bring pineapple and sugar to boil. Add jello and stir until dissolved. Add water and congeal partially. Add cheese. Fold in thawed whipped topping and nuts. Pour in container and chill until firm.

Yield: 4-6 servings

Judy Grant

Two Bean Salad
with Balsamic Vinaigrette

1   (14 ounce) can chick peas, drained
1   (14 ounce) can black beans, drained
⅔   cup chopped red onion

¼   cup chopped parsley
3   tablespoons olive oil
3   tablespoons balsamic vinegar
3   cloves garlic, chopped

Mix all ingredients. Refrigerate.

Yield: 6-8 servings

Dina Trimboli Whitley, class of 80

Black Bean Salad

4 tablespoons chopped cilantro	2 tablespoons olive oil
1 clove garlic, minced	4 tablespoons balsamic vinegar
1 jalapeño (or to taste), chopped	salt and pepper to taste
2 teaspoons grated lemon peel	ground cumin to taste
3 cans black beans, rinsed and drained	

In a glass or stainless steel bowl, mix cilantro, garlic, jalapeño and lemon peel. Add beans, olive oil and vinegar. Toss gingerly to coat. Add seasonings to taste. Will keep several days in the refrigerator.

Yield: 8-10 servings

Lisa Mumford Kluttz, class of 88

Julie's Bean Salad

1 (15 ounce) can sliced green beans, drained	1 cup chopped celery
1 (15 ounce) can shoepeg corn, drained	1 cup chopped onion
	1 green pepper, chopped
1 (15 ounce) can small peas, drained	1 medium jar diced pimentos, drained

Marinade:

1 cup sugar	1 tablespoon salt
½ cup oil	coarsely ground black pepper to taste
¾ cup tarragon or regular vinegar	

Combine all vegetables in large bowl. Combine all marinade ingredients in blender. Pour over vegetables. Refrigerate several hours before serving. Will stay fresh in refrigerator for one week.

Yield: 8-10 servings

Lynda Blount

Corn and Black Bean Salad

1	(16 ounce) can black beans, drained	½	cup sliced green onions
1	(8 ounce) can whole kernel corn, drained	1	red pepper, diced
		¾	cup salsa
4	ounces Monterey Jack cheese, cubed or shredded	1	tablespoon olive oil
		2	tablespoons lemon juice
		2	teaspoons ground cumin

Combine first five ingredients in large bowl. Combine remaining ingredients and mix well. Toss with bean mixture. Cover and chill. Best if made a day ahead. Recipe can be doubled for large crowds.

Yield: 8 servings

Marti Mostellar

Green Bean and Beet Salad

2	(15 ounce) cans green beans	1	large onion, thinly sliced
1	(15 ounce) can sliced beets		

Dressing:

¼	cup vegetable oil	¼	teaspoon pepper
¾	cup sugar	⅔	cup vinegar
1	teaspoon salt	½	cup water
1	clove garlic, minced		

Drain vegetables. Set aside. Make dressing and put in saucepan. Add beets. Boil 5 minutes. Remove from heat. Add drained beans and onions. Stir well. Refrigerate 12 hours before serving, stirring several times. May be kept one week in refrigerator.

Yield: 6-8 servings

Sarah Edwards

Broccoli Salad

1	pound bacon
3	bunches broccoli, cut into florets
½	cup raisins
½	cup sunflower seeds

1	medium onion, finely chopped
½	cup fat-free mayonnaise
½	cup sugar
2	teaspoons vinegar

Fry bacon until crisp, drain, crumble and set aside. In large bowl combine next four ingredients. In small bowl mix remaining ingredients until well blended. Spoon over broccoli mixture and toss well to coat. Sprinkle with bacon and toss. Cover and refrigerate at least 3 hours - better overnight.

Yield: 6-8 servings

Kathy White

Broccoli-Orange Salad

4	cups fresh broccoli florets
1	small purple onion, thinly sliced
½	cup raisins
½	cup pecan pieces, toasted
¼	cup mayonnaise

¼	cup sugar
1½	tablespoons white vinegar
1	(11 ounce) can mandarin oranges, drained

Combine first four ingredients in a bowl. Set aside. Combine mayonnaise, sugar and vinegar. Add to broccoli mixture, stirring to coat. Gently stir in mandarin oranges. Cover and refrigerate at least 3 hours.

Yield: 6 servings

Jenette Low

Low-Fat Red, White and Green Salad

½ cup fat-free sour cream
½ cup fat-free mayonnaise or salad
    dressing
⅛ teaspoon salt
⅛ teaspoon pepper

2½ cups broccoli florets
2½ cups cauliflower florets
4-5 roma tomatoes, chopped
¼   cup onion, finely chopped

Mix first four ingredients well for dressing. Combine the vegetables and toss gently with dressing. Chill several hours before serving.

Yield: 10-12 servings

Ada Nunn

Summer Vegetable Salad

3 yellow squash
3 cucumbers
3 carrots
1 medium green pepper
1 medium red pepper
1 medium onion

¾ cup sugar
½ cup balsamic vinegar (or cider
    vinegar)
¼ cup olive oil
1 tablespoon mustard seed

Thinly slice squash, cucumbers and carrots. Dice peppers and onions. Mix all vegetables in a large glass bowl. Mix last four ingredients well in a small bowl. Pour over vegetables. Cover with plastic wrap and refrigerate several hours before serving. Will keep several days in the refrigerator.

Yield: 6-8 servings

Lisa Mumford Kluttz, class of 88

Curried Rice Salad

1 package flavored rice, cooked according to directions omitting butter	1 jar marinated artichoke hearts, sliced, reserving marinade
¼ cup sliced stuffed olives	⅓ cup mayonnaise or salad dressing
½ cup chopped spring onions	½ teaspoon curry powder
½ cup chopped green peppers	

Prepare rice. Mix with olives, onions, peppers and artichoke hearts. Combine marinade, mayonnaise and curry powder. Pour over other ingredients and toss well. Refrigerate several hours before serving.

Yield: 4-6 servings

Kay Gross

Caesar Butterflies

⅓ cup red wine vinegar	½ pound butterfly pasta, cooked al dente
2 teaspoons Dijon style mustard	
1 clove garlic, minced	8 cups mixed salad greens
pinch of sugar	2 cups peeled, quartered and cubed cucumbers
coarse salt to taste	
½ cup olive oil	1 cup coarsely chopped walnuts
freshly ground black pepper to taste	2 ounces fresh Parmesan cheese

Prepare dressing in a small bowl by whisking together vinegar, mustard, garlic, sugar and salt. Slowly drizzle oil, whisking constantly until slightly thickened. Season with pepper to taste. Place cooked pasta in a large bowl and toss with 3 tablespoons dressing. Just before serving add greens, cucumbers and walnuts. Toss with 4 tablespoons dressing, more if desired. Season with additional salt and pepper and toss again. With a vegetable peeler, shave thin slices of Parmesan atop salad or grate coarsely. Serve immediately.

Yield: 6-8 servings

Dina Trimboli Whitley, class of 80

Pasta Salad

1 (12 ounce) bag garden style twirl pasta
3 pickling sized cucumbers, peeled and diced
1 (6 ounce) can crabmeat, drained
1 (5 ounce) container boiled ham or honey ham, diced
8 ounces fat-free creamy Italian dressing
2-4 tablespoons mayonnaise
½ cup pickle relish or cubes
5 ounces frozen green peas
salt and pepper to taste

Cook pasta according to directions. When done, cool by running under cold water in colander. Drain thoroughly and mix with other ingredients. Chill thoroughly.

Yield: 6-8 servings

Eugenia Briley

Terrific Tortellini Salad

2 (14 ounce) packages frozen cheese tortellini
1 green bell pepper, chopped
1 red bell pepper, chopped
1 cucumber, chopped
1 (14 ounce) can artichoke hearts, drained and rinsed
1 (8 ounce) bottle Caesar salad dressing
1 (8 ounce) package crumbled feta cheese
1 tomato cut into wedges

Prepare tortellini according to directions. Drain. Rinse under cold water and drain. In large bowl combine tortellini, peppers, cucumber, artichoke hearts, dressing and feta cheese. Cover and refrigerate 2 hours. When ready to serve mix well and arrange tomato wedges as garnish.

Yield: 8-10 servings

Faith Greenwood

Tortellini Salad

1   bag cheese tortellini
1   bottle robust flavor Italian
    dressing
1   container crumbled feta cheese

2   tomatoes, cut into bite sized
    pieces
2   small cans sliced black olives
1   can artichoke hearts, cut into
    bite sized pieces

Cook tortellini and rinse under cold water. Mix in tomatoes, olives and artichoke hearts. Mix in dressing. Top with feta cheese. Serve chilled.

Yield: 8 servings

Lisa Williams Merriam, class of 78

Artichoke and Tuna Salad

2   large cans white tuna packed in
    spring water
4   ribs celery, washed and diced
2/3 cup artichoke relish
1/3 cup sweet pickle relish

1   tablespoon parsley
1/2 cup mayonnaise
4   packs artificial sweetener
1   teaspoon lemon juice

Combine all ingredients and chill.

Yield: 8-10 servings

Ella Rodgman

Chicken Salad

3   cups diced chicken
2   cups finely chopped celery
3/4 cup mayonnaise

2   cups seedless white grapes
1   cup chopped red delicious apples
1   small package slivered almonds

Toss all ingredients, saving almonds to sprinkle on top. Delicious served in puff pastry shells or lettuce cups with fruit salad, fruit gelatin mold or tomato aspic.

Yield: 12 servings

Kathy White

Chinese Marinated Vegetable Salad

1 (17 ounce) can peas, drained
1 (15½ ounce) can French style
   green beans, drained
1 (12 ounce) can shoe peg corn,
   drained
1 (5 ounce) can water chestnuts,
   sliced and drained

1 (4 ounce) can mushrooms,
   sliced and drained
1 (2 ounce) jar chopped pimento
1 small head cauliflower, broken
   into florets
1 cup chopped green pepper
1 purple or Vidalia onion, thinly
   sliced

Marinade:

2½ cups cider vinegar
2   cups sugar

1 tablespoon salt
¼ teaspoon pepper

In a BIG bowl combine all salad ingredients, pour marinade over top
and toss. Cover tightly and let sit in refrigerator at least 72 hours.
Excellent for a week at the beach or a family reunion.

Yield: A LOT!!

Cathy Green

Chinese Salad

1 head NAPA cabbage (not bok
   choy)
5 green onions, diced
3 (2.8 ounce) packages dried soup
   noodles
½ cup sesame seeds

½ cup slivered almonds
1 cup sugar
½ cup salad oil
2 tablespoons soy sauce
½ cup vinegar
¼ cup sesame oil

Chop cabbage coarsely. Add diced onions. Break up noodles and
place on cookie sheet. Toast lightly then add to cabbage and onions.
In a skillet, cook almonds and sesame seeds until light brown. Add to
cabbage mixture. In separate small bowl combine sugar, oils, soy
sauce and vinegar. Blend well and pour over salad. Chill at least 2
hours.

Yield: 6-8 servings

Martha Flowers

Oriental Cabbage Salad

2-3 chicken breasts, seasoned with
     garlic salt and pepper
1   large head cabbage, sliced and
     chopped
3-4 green onions, chopped

4   tablespoons toasted sesame seeds
4   tablespoons toasted slivered
     almonds
3   (2.8 ounce) packages chicken
     flavored dried noodle soup

Dressing:

7½   tablespoons sugar
⅜   cup oil (1½ tablespoons sesame
     oil plus amount of vegetable oil
     to equal ⅜ cup)
½   teaspoon MSG (optional)
2   teaspoons salt
¼-½ teaspoon pepper

⅜   cup rice vinegar (may add
     more)
3   tablespoons fresh lemon juice
1   tablespoon grated fresh ginger or
     1½ teaspoons bottled
1½   packages seasoning from the
     dried noodle soup

Boil chicken breasts 30 minutes. Cool and shred. Combine chicken, cabbage and onions. Refrigerate. Mix dressing ingredients well. Break up dried noodles. Toss all together and refrigerate 1-2 hours. Will keep 3 days. You may substitute ham or turkey for chicken.

Yield: 4-6 servings

Carole Cameron

River Runner Chicken Salad

1   (10 ounce) can chicken,
     drained
1   (15 ounce) can light red kidney
     beans, drained
1½   cups grated cheddar cheese

2   tomatoes, diced
6   tablespoons mayonnaise
2   avocados, sliced
     salt and pepper to taste
     pita bread

Mix all ingredients, except avocados and pita bread. Put avocado slices in pita bread and then stuff with chicken salad.

Yield: 8 servings

Holly Hill

Creamy Turkey Salad

²/₃ cup sour cream
1⅓ cups mayonnaise
4 cups roasted turkey, chopped
½ cup chopped scallions
¾ cup chopped celery

2 tablespoons sweet pickle cubes, drained well
1 cup roasted pistachios
salt and pepper to taste

Combine sour cream and mayonnaise, blending well. Stir in turkey until well coated. Sprinkle remaining ingredients over the top of the turkey. Mix and refrigerate.

Yield: 4 servings

Dina Trimboli Whitley, class of 80

Seafood Pasta Salad

1 pound raw shrimp, shelled
1 pound raw bay scallops
½ pound lump crabmeat
1 pound pasta (bowtie is good)
1 cup tiny peas, fresh or frozen
½ cup sweet diced red pepper
½ cup minced Bermuda onion

½ cup olive oil
3-4 tablespoons lemon juice
½ cup basil puree
1 teaspoon salt
½ teaspoon pepper
1 cup sliced black olives (optional)

Drop scallops and shrimp in large pot of boiling water. Boil 1 minute and drain. Cook pasta according to directions. Drain and rinse under cold water. Toss drained seafood and crabmeat with pasta. Add peas, red pepper and onions. Toss again. In small bowl whisk lemon juice, olive oil, basil puree, salt and pepper. Pour over salad and toss again. Scatter olives on top. Serve at room temperature.

Basil Puree:
3 cups basil leaves or 3 cups fresh parsley

1 tablespoon dried basil
3 tablespoons olive oil

Blend, cover and refrigerate.

Yield: 12-15 servings

Frances Parrott

Ham, White Grape and Pasta Salad

2 ½ inch thick slices boiled ham,
   cubed
1 cup white seedless grapes

1 bag tricolored spiral pasta,
   cooked, drained and cooled
1 tablespoon dried onions

Dressing:
1 cup sour cream
½ cup mayonnaise
3 tablespoons white vinegar

8 packs artificial sweetener
1 tablespoon dill

Combine first four ingredients in large bowl and set aside. Mix together dressing ingredients and pour over pasta mixture. Mix well and chill 1 hour before serving.

Yield: 8 servings

Shelia Hobgood

Hot Portobella Mushroom Salad

1 head green or red leaf lettuce,
   washed and torn for salad bites
1 package portobella mushrooms
   sliced into large pieces
1 teaspoon balsamic vinegar

1 teaspoon olive oil
½ cup prepared Italian dressing
   crumbled bleu or feta cheese,
   optional but recommended

Prepare lettuce and refrigerate. In a nonstick skillet, heat dressing, vinegar, oil and mushrooms over medium-high heat for about 4-5 minutes or until mushrooms brown. Stir to make sure mushrooms get even heat. Remove from heat and place mushrooms over lettuce, spooning approximately 1 teaspoon of dressing sauce over mushrooms and lettuce. Add crumbled cheese and serve immediately. About mushrooms: They should never be allowed to sit in water. Clean by damp-sponging or running under cool water and quickly blotting dry with paper towels.

Yield: 4 servings

Jo Allen, class of 76

Shrimp Salad

3   pounds medium shrimp
2   green bell peppers
1   large onion
2   boiled eggs
1   rib celery

3   heaping tablespoons horseradish
½   cup mayonnaise
½   cup dressing
juice of ½ lemon

Boil shrimp. Peel, devein and chop into small pieces. Chop onion, bell pepper and celery. Add remaining ingredients. Mix well. Chill one hour. Serve on lettuce.

Yield: 8-10 servings

Laura O'Brien

Parrott Yard Sale Taco Salad

1   pound hamburger, browned and
    drained
1   package taco seasoning mix
½   cup water
1   head lettuce, torn into pieces
2   large tomatoes, chopped
2   cups grated cheddar cheese

2   cans kidney beans, drained
    (1 light, 1 dark)
1   small bag corn chips, broken
    into pieces
1   small bottle Catalina dressing
1   medium onion, chopped
black olives
sour cream

Cook first three ingredients until water is gone, stirring frequently. Mix all remaining ingredients with beef mixture, reserving chopped onion, black olives and sour cream as garnish.

Yield: 6-8 servings

Margie Castleberry

Breads
&
Muffins

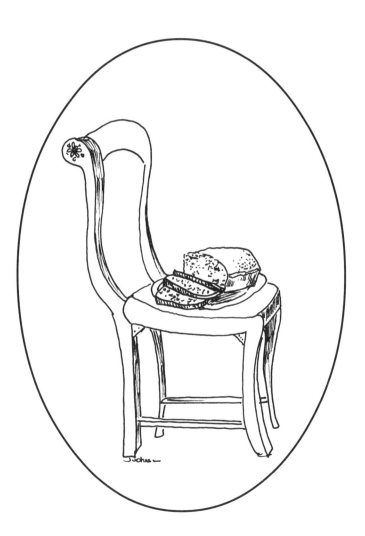

Apricot Banana Bread

⅓ cup butter or margarine, softened	1 teaspoon baking powder
⅔ cup sugar	½ teaspoon baking soda
2 eggs	½ teaspoon salt
1 cup mashed ripe bananas (2-3 medium)	1 cup 100% bran cereal (not flakes)
¼ cup buttermilk	¾ cup chopped dried apricots
1¼ cups all purpose flour	½ cup chopped walnuts

In mixing bowl, cream butter and sugar. Add eggs. Mix well. Combine bananas and buttermilk and add to creamed mixture. Combine flour, baking powder, baking soda and salt. Add to creamed mixture. Stir in bran, apricots and walnuts. Pour into greased 9x5x3 inch loaf pan. Bake at 350 for 55-60 minutes or until bread tests done. Cool 10 minutes. Remove from pan to a wire rack.

Yield: 1 loaf

Cathy Wellman

Banana Nut Bread

¾ cup margarine	1½ teaspoon salt
2¼ cups sugar	1½ cups banana pulp (4-6 ripe bananas)
3 eggs	6 tablespoons buttermilk (do not use nonfat)
1½ teaspoons vanilla	¾ cup chopped pecans
3 cups cake flour (plain)	
¾ teaspoon baking soda	

Cream margarine and sugar. Add eggs and vanilla. Sift together dry ingredients. Mix like cake batter, adding flour mixture alternately with buttermilk and banana pulp to margarine mixture. Add pecans and pour into two loaf pans. Bake at 350 for approximately 1 hour. These store and freeze beautifully.

Yield: 2 loaves

Banana Bread

½	cup shortening	1¼	cups sifted cake flour
1	cup sugar	¾	teaspoon baking soda
2	eggs	½	teaspoon salt
¾	cup mashed, ripe bananas		

Cream shortening and sugar until light. Add eggs, one at a time, beating well after each. Stir in bananas. Sift together dry ingredients. Add to banana mixture. Mix until well blended. Pour into greased loaf pan. Bake at 350 for 45 minutes. May also be baked in mini loaf pans for variety or gift giving.

Lisa Britt Carrigan, class of 81

Bayou Banana Bread

½	cup margarine	½	teaspoon salt
¾	cup sugar	½	teaspoon cinnamon
2	eggs	¼	teaspoon ground allspice
1	teaspoon vanilla	¼	teaspoon cloves
2	cups flour	5	mashed bananas
1½	teaspoons baking powder	½	cup walnuts, optional
½	teaspoon baking soda		

Cream margarine and sugar until light and fluffy. Blend in eggs and vanilla. Add combined dry ingredients to creamed mixture alternately with bananas, mixing well after each addition. Stir in nuts. Pour into greased and floured loaf pan. Bake at 350 for 55-60 minutes. This is great baked in muffin cups also.

Yield: 1 loaf

Kathy White

Easy Biscotti

2	eggs	1	teaspoon flavoring (lemon,
⅔	cup sugar		almond, vanilla or anise)
		1	cup flour

Beat eggs and sugar thoroughly. Add flavoring and mix together. Mix in flour and pour mixture into greased and floured loaf pan. Bake at 375 about 20 minutes or until a toothpick comes out clean. The pan will only be half full. Remove from pan and cut into 16 one half inch slices. Place slices on greased baking sheet. Bake 5 minutes or until lightly browned. Turn and bake an additional 5 minutes until lightly browned. Keep in airtight container.

Yield: 16 servings

Linda Peacock

Six Week Bran Muffins

2	cups boiling water	4	cups bran flakes
2	cups bran cereal	5	cups flour, sifted
1	cup oil	5	teaspoons soda
3	cups sugar	1	teaspoon salt
2	eggs		raisins, dates or nuts, optional
1	quart buttermilk		

Pour boiling water over bran cereal. Let sit. Cream oil, sugar, eggs and buttermilk. Add bran flakes. Gradually add sifted flour, soda and salt. Fold in soaked bran cereal. Bake in paper-lined muffin tins at 400 for 20 minutes. (Use ice cream scoop to quickly put batter in lined muffin pan.) Batter keeps in refrigerator for six weeks.

Joyce Witherington Mattux,
Sea Island Beach Club Spa, class of 77

Anita's Sour Cream Cornbread

1	box cornbread mix	½	stick margarine, melted
1	(8 ounce) container sour cream	1	(16 ounce) can cream style corn
3	eggs		

Mix ingredients and pour into a greased 9x12 inch casserole dish. Bake at 350 for 35 minutes. Let cool. Will not be set completely.

Yield: 8-10 servings

Anita Watson

Cornbread

2	eggs	1	(16 ounce) can creamed corn
1	cup sour cream	1	box corn meal mix
⅓	cup cooking oil		

Mix all together and pour into greased baking dish. Bake at 400 for 30 minutes.

Margie Castleberry

Cornbread

1	box corn muffin mix	1	egg
1	small can cream style corn	1	stick butter, melted
1	small container sour cream	1	tablespoon red pepper, minced

Combine all ingredients. Stir well and pour into casserole dish. Bake at 350 for one hour.

Yield: 15-20 servings

Spoon Cornbread

8	ounces creamed corn	½	cup butter
8	ounces kernel corn	2	eggs
8	ounces sour cream		

Mix and pour into 11x7 inch greased pan. Bake at 350 for 35 minutes.

Linda Collins recipe submitted by Kay Gross

Charlie's Cornbread

1	cup corn meal	1½	teaspoons salt
½	cup corn oil	1	cup cream style corn
3	teaspoons baking powder	1	cup sour cream
2	eggs		

Mix ingredients until blended. Pour into 8x8x2 inch dish and bake at 400 for 30 minutes.

Yield: 9 servings

Linda McMullen

Old Virginia Spoon Bread

1	cup corn meal	3	tablespoons butter, melted
½	teaspoon salt	3	eggs, beaten
2	cups water	1	cup ice cold milk

Stir corn meal and salt into water, then bring to boil and cook one minute. Remove from heat and add melted butter. Stir in egg. Add ice cold milk to mixture and stir. Pour into hot buttered 2 quart casserole. Bake at 425 for 25 minutes.

Yield: 6 servings

Nancy B. W. Bowers

Jalapeño Cornbread

2	cups cornmeal	½	cup salad oil or bacon drippings
2	teaspoons sugar	2	eggs, well beaten
1	teaspoon salt	1	(17 ounce) can cream style corn
½	teaspoon baking soda	2-3	jalapeño peppers, finely chopped
½	teaspoon baking powder	1	onion, chopped
¾	cup buttermilk	1½	cups grated sharp cheese

Combine dry ingredients. Add remaining ingredients, stirring until all ingredients are moistened. Pour into hot, greased 9x13x2 inch baking pan. Bake at 400 for 45-55 minutes or until browned.

Yield: 15 servings

Ella Rodgman

Corn Muffins

1	box cornbread mix	1	can cream style corn
2	eggs	1	stick butter
8	ounces sour cream		

Mix and bake at 350 for 45 minutes. Great with chili.

Yield: 12 large muffins

Marti Mostellar

Eggbread (Old Fashioned Spoonbread)

1	cup cornmeal	2	teaspoons margarine or butter
2	cups water	2	eggs, beaten
¼	teaspoon salt	1	cup milk

Preheat oven to 325 and place casserole dish in oven until margarine has melted. Combine first four ingredients and place in saucepan over medium heat until mixture thickens. Add eggs and milk. Pour into baking dish and bake for 45 minutes. This goes well with grilled chicken or fish.

Nancy Deichmann

Grandma Cobb's Cranberry Bread

2	cups flour		grated rind and juice of 1 orange
½	teaspoon salt	1	egg
1½	teaspoons baking powder	1	cup chopped nuts (walnuts are best)
½	teaspoon baking soda		
1	cup sugar	1	cup cranberries (measure first and then cut cranberries into fourths)
2	tablespoons butter (add hot water to make ¾ cup liquid)		

Sift flour, salt, baking powder, baking soda and sugar. Add hot water with butter. Combine grated rind and juice with beaten egg. Add to dry ingredients, carefully blending. Fold in nuts and cranberries. Bake at 350 for about 30 minutes.

Ruth Mollison

Thanksgiving Famous Cranberry Bread

2 cups all purpose flour	1 egg, beaten
1 cup sugar	1 teaspoon grated orange peel
1½ teaspoons baking soda	¾ cup orange juice
1 teaspoon salt	1½ cups light raisins
½ teaspoon baking powder	1½ cups fresh or canned cranberries
¼ cup butter, softened	

Sift flour, sugar, baking soda, salt and baking powder in large bowl. Cut butter into dry ingredients until crumbly. Add eggs, orange peel, and orange juice all at once to flour mixture. Stir only until mixture is evenly moist. Fold in raisins and cranberries. Turn into a greased 9x5x3 inch loaf pan. Bake 1 hour at 350 or until cake tester comes out clean. Remove from oven, cool and serve.

T. A. Smith's Great-great Grandmother Richardson

Cranberry Bread

1½ cups fresh cranberries	¼ cup butter
2 cups all purpose flour	1 egg, beaten
1 cup sugar	1 teaspoon orange rind, grated
1½ teaspoons baking powder	¾ cup orange juice
½ teaspoon soda	1½ cups golden raisins
1 teaspoon salt	

Wash and drain cranberries. Grind coarsely. Set aside. Combine flour, sugar, baking powder, soda and salt in a large mixing bowl. Cut in butter with a pastry blender until mixture resembles coarse crumbs. Add egg, orange rind and juice. Stir in raisins and cranberries. Spoon into a greased and floured loaf pan. Bake at 350 for 1 hour.

Nancy B. W. Bowers

Doggie Biscuits

1	teaspoon instant beef bouillon	1	(3¼ ounce) jar bacon flavored
½	cup hot water		bits
2¼	cups whole wheat flour	1	tablespoon firmly packed brown
½	cup nonfat dry milk		sugar
⅓	cup vegetable oil	1	egg

In a medium bowl, dissolve bouillon in water. Add remaining ingredients, stirring until well blended. On a lightly floured surface, use a floured rolling pin to roll out dough to ⅛ inch thickness. Use a 2 inch heart shaped cookie cutter to cut out dough. Transfer to a greased baking sheet. Bake at 300 for 30-35 minutes or until firm. Transfer to a wire rack to cool completely. Store in an airtight container.

Yield: about six dozen doggie biscuits

The children will love to make these for their dog and their dog's friends!

Carla Lancaster

Cheese Biscuit Snacks

1	pound extra sharp cheddar cheese, grated	2	cups self-rising flour
½	cup butter or margarine, softened	¼-½	teaspoon ground red pepper

Mix cheese and butter until blended. Mix in flour and red pepper until dough forms (if dry work with hands). Turn onto a lightly floured board and roll or pat into ½ inch thickness. Cut with 1½ inch biscuit cutter. Place one inch apart on ungreased cookie sheet. Bake at 350 until edges just begin to brown and crust is dry to the touch, approximately 10-12 minutes. Immediately remove from cookie sheet to cool. Store in airtight container up to 3 days. Freeze up to 1 month.

Samia Garner

Cheesy Italian Bread

1	loaf French or Italian style bread	1	cup grated sharp cheddar cheese
½	cup mayonnaise	1	cup finely chopped green onions

Slice loaf in half lengthwise. Spread mayonnaise on each and top with cheese and onions. Broil until bubbly. Slice and serve. Great with salads.

Faith Greenwood

Cheese-Garlic Biscuits

2	cups buttermilk baking mix	¼	cup butter or margarine, melted
⅔	cup milk	½	teaspoon garlic powder
½	cup shredded cheddar cheese		

Mix first three ingredients well. Stir vigorously 30 seconds. Drop dough by heaping tablespoons onto an ungreased cookie sheet. Bake in a preheated 450 oven for 8-10 minutes or until golden brown. Combine butter and garlic powder. Brush over warm biscuits before removing from cookie sheet. Serve warm.

Yield: 10-12 biscuits

Dawn Davis

Butterscotch Monkey Bread

½	cup nuts	¾	cup brown sugar
1	package frozen dough balls	¾	teaspoon cinnamon
1	package butterscotch pudding mix		Or: vanilla pudding, ¾ cup regular sugar, 1 teaspoon vanilla
1	stick butter, melted		

Sprinkle nuts in bottom of greased Bundt pan. Add 22 frozen dough balls. Sprinkle pudding mix over balls. Combine butter, sugar and cinnamon. Pour over dough balls. Cover and put in unheated oven overnight. Uncover and bake at 350 for 25-30 minutes. Invert immediately and serve warm.

Cindy Archie

Gingerbread

1	cup butter, softened	1½	teaspoons baking soda
1	cup granulated sugar	1	teaspoon ginger
1	cup molasses	1	teaspoon cinnamon
1	cup boiling water	1	teaspoon nutmeg
2½	cups all purpose flour	3	eggs
1	teaspoon salt		

Place first three ingredients in mixing bowl. Add boiling water, stirring until butter has melted. Set aside to cool. Sift dry ingredients together. Set aside. When molasses mixture is cooled, beat in eggs with mixer. Blend in dry ingredients, mixing until smooth. Pour batter into greased 9x13 inch pan. Bake at 325 for one hour.

Yield: 16 servings

Leraine Collier

Pumpkin Bread

3	cups sugar	1½	teaspoons nutmeg
4	eggs	1	teaspoon cloves
1	cup vegetable oil	2	teaspoons salt
1	can pumpkin	1½	teaspoons cinnamon
3½	cups sifted all purpose flour	1½	teaspoons allspice
2	teaspoons baking soda	⅔	cup water
1	teaspoon baking powder		nonstick cooking spray

Blend sugar, eggs and oil thoroughly. Stir together all dry ingredients and add to sugar mixture. Mix well. Add water and mix well. Spray three loaf pans with nonstick cooking spray. Pour mixture evenly into pans and bake at 325 approximately 1 hour. Allow to cool in pans 15 minutes then remove from pans to wire rack. Freezes well. Batter can be used for muffins also.

Yield: 3 loaves

Kathy White

Homemade Louisiana Yeast Rolls

1	package dry yeast (do not use rapid rise variety)	4	tablespoons oil
1	cup warm water	2	tablespoons sugar
⅛	teaspoon salt	2½-3 cups flour	

In large mixing bowl, combine yeast with warm water and dissolve completely. Add salt, oil and sugar. Slowly mix by hand or with dough hooks on mixer, 1 cup of flour at time. Continue to add flour until a soft ball forms. If mixing by hand knead one minute. Place in bowl and cover with cloth to rise in draft free area for 1½ to 2 hours. Put out on floured board. Knead but do not over work. Press all air out to about 2½ inch thickness. Cut rolls with small glass cutter coated with oil. Place in pan, coating tops of rolls with oil. Cover with plastic wrap and refrigerate two hours or freeze for several weeks. Take from refrigerator one hour before baking. Bake at 375 for 20-25 minutes.

Gloria Smith

Lemon Tea Bread

6	tablespoons butter	½	cup milk (may use part lemon juice)
1	cup sugar		grated rind of 1 lemon
2	eggs	½	cup chopped walnuts, dusted with flour
1½	cups plain flour		
1½	teaspoons baking powder		
¼	teaspoon salt		

Glaze:

⅓	cup sugar	juice of 1 lemon

Cream butter, sugar and eggs. Set aside. Combine flour, baking powder and salt. Add to egg mixture. Add milk and rind to mixture. Stir well. Add nuts and stir just until mixed. Bake approximately 40 minutes at 325. Combine sugar and lemon for glaze and pour over warm bread while still in pans. Cool slightly before removing from pans.

Samia Garner

Sourdough Bread

6	cups bread flour	½	cup corn oil
½	cup sugar	1½	cups warm water
1	tablespoon salt	1	teaspoon vanilla
1	cup starter	1	teaspoon milk

Sift flour, sugar and salt together in large bowl. Mix starter, oil, water, vanilla and milk. Mix together until a good bread dough forms. Grease large bowl. Put dough in bowl and grease top. Cover with plastic wrap and a towel and let rise 8 to 12 hours. (I put mine under stairwell with hot water heater.) Punch down (should have doubled in bulk) and knead a little. Divide into three loaves and knead each 8-12 times. Place in greased loaf pans, grease tops and make tent with bath towel. Let rise another 8 to 12 hours. Bake at 325-350 for 35-40 minutes or until golden.

Sourdough Starter:

1	package yeast, dissolved in	2½	tablespoons plain flour
	½ cup lukewarm water	3	tablespoons instant potato flakes
2	tablespoons sugar	¾	cup sugar
2	cups warm water	1	cup warm water

Mix together the 2 tablespoons sugar, 2 cups warm water and plain flour. Add the yeast mixture to this. Place in a warm, dark place and let stand for 5 days. Feed every 3 to 5 days with the instant potato flakes, ¾ cup sugar and 1 cup warm water. Let stand out all day. Remove 1 cup and return remainder to refrigerator.

It's best to find someone with starter and get it from them, but the above starter does work.

Judy Johnson

Judy's Coffee Cake

Sourdough Bread dough after first rising   *almond, poppy or other flavor filling*

Roll out dough to about 16x12 inches. Spread ½ can of filling and roll up. Seal seams. Place on greased baking sheet and rise 8-12 hours. Bake at 325-350 for 35-40 minutes or until golden.

Judy Johnson

Pumpkin Bread

1½	cups sugar	1⅔	cups sifted flour
1	teaspoon cinnamon	1	teaspoon baking soda
1	teaspoon nutmeg	1	teaspoon salt
1	teaspoon ginger	1	cup canned pumpkin
1	teaspoon cloves	2	eggs
1	teaspoon allspice	½	cup cooking oil
½	cup raisins	½	cup water
¼	teaspoon baking powder	½	cup chopped nuts

Combine dry ingredients and mix everything into dry ingredients. Bake one hour at 350. This is easy and keeps a long time.

Evelyn Deane

Zucchini Bread

3	eggs, well beaten	3	cups flour
1	cup vegetable oil	1	teaspoon salt
2	cups sugar	¼	teaspoon baking powder
2	cups zucchini, grated and drained well	1	teaspoon baking soda
		¾	teaspoon nutmeg
1	teaspoon vanilla	1	tablespoon cinnamon

Mix together eggs, oil, sugar, zucchini and vanilla. Sift together dry ingredients. Add dry ingredients to egg mixture. Pour into two greased and floured loaf pans. Bake at 350 for approximately 55 minutes or until center springs back when touched lightly. Cool 15 minutes and remove from pans. Cool completely on wire racks before wrapping. Freezes well.

Faith Greenwood

Pasta, Rice & Vegetarian

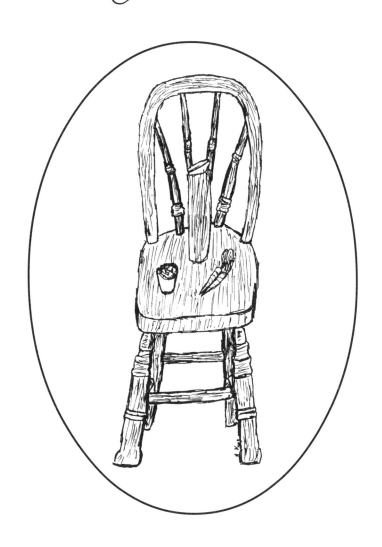

Dressing

½	stalk celery, chopped	1	loaf bread
1	onion, chopped	1	bag dry stuffing mix
¼	cup margarine	2	eggs
1	box crushed corn flakes	4	cups turkey or chicken broth

Sauté celery and onion in margarine. Combine remaining ingredients with celery and onion. Place in a greased baking pan. Bake at 400 until brown on top. This is the tasty dressing you will find in the Arendell Parrott Academy cafeteria on Turkey Day and other special occasions!

Sue Haddock

Manicotti

1	cup shredded mozzarella cheese	fresh basil
1	cup ricotta cheese	cooked manicotti shells
½	cup Parmesan cheese	spaghetti sauce
2	eggs, beaten	

Combine cheeses, eggs and basil. Stuff cooked shells. Cover bottom of 3 quart baking dish with sauce. Place shells on top of sauce then cover with remaining sauce. Bake at 350 for 30-35 minutes. Serve with salad and garlic bread.

Kim Stokes

Parmesan Oven Rice

⅔	cup rice	2	teaspoons chicken bouillon
1⅔	cups water		granules
4	tablespoons margarine	¼-½	cup Parmesan cheese

Combine all ingredients in a 2 quart casserole. Bake covered at 375 for 45 minutes.

Yield: 4 servings

Lisa Hines

Quick Kid Casserole

1	pound lean ground beef, browned and drained	1	package dried onion soup mix
2	cups cooked rice	1	(6 ounce) can sweet peas, drained
2	(15 ounce) cans stewed Italian tomatoes, drained	2	cups shredded cheddar cheese

Combine beef, rice, tomatoes and soup mix. Stir to mix well. Fold in peas. Pour into a two quart casserole and top with cheese. Bake at 350 for 30 minutes.

Yield: 4-6 servings

Karen Williams

Rice Casserole

1	stick margarine, melted	1½	cups long grain rice
2	stalks celery, chopped	1	can mushrooms
1	package slivered almonds	2	cans beef bouillon or broth

Cook celery and almonds in butter for three minutes. Add rice and mushrooms and cook one minute longer. Add bouillon or broth and place in a covered dish. Bake at 300 for 1 hour.

Ella Rodgman

Broccoli and Rice Casserole

1	package flavored country rice	1	(10¾ ounce) can cream of mushroom soup
1	(10 ounce) package frozen chopped broccoli, thawed and drained	4-6	ounces grated cheese

Cook rice according to package directions. Blend in broccoli and soup. Place in casserole dish and top with grated cheese. Bake at 350 for 20 minutes or until hot. Fast and easy!

Laura O'Brien

Savannah Red Rice

¼ pound bacon
½ cup chopped onion
2 cups rice, uncooked
2 (16 ounce) cans tomatoes

3 teaspoons salt
¼ teaspoon pepper
⅛ teaspoon hot sauce

In large frying pan, fry bacon until crisp. Remove from pan, crumble and reserve. Sauté onions in bacon grease until tender. Add rice, tomatoes, bacon and seasonings. Cook on top of stove for 10 minutes. Pour into large, greased casserole dish. Cover tightly and bake at 350 for 1 hour.

Yield: 8 servings

Linda McMullen

French Rice

1 (10½ ounce) can onion soup, undiluted
½ cup butter or margarine, melted
1 (4½ ounce) jar sliced mushrooms, undrained

1 (8 ounce) can sliced water chestnuts, undrained
1 cup uncooked regular rice

Combine soup and butter. Stir well. Drain mushrooms and water chestnuts, reserving liquid. Add enough water to reserved liquid to equal 1⅓ cups. Add mushrooms, water chestnuts, liquid and rice to soup mixture. Stir well. Pour into a lightly greased 10x6x2 inch baking dish. Cover and bake at 350 for one hour.

Yield: 6 servings

Kay Gross

Green Rice Casserole

1	stick margarine	1	package chopped broccoli, cooked
½	cup chopped onions		and drained
½	cup chopped celery	1	cup rice, cooked
1	can cream of celery soup	1	cup grated cheddar cheese
1	(8 ounce) jar processed cheese		
	product		

Sauté onions and celery in margarine. Stir in soup, cheese product, broccoli and rice. Cover with grated cheddar cheese. Bake in low oven for 20-30 minutes.

Yield: 6-8 servings

Betty Andrews

Wild Rice Casserole

½	stick margarine	1	medium onion, diced or 1
1	can beef broth		tablespoon dried minced onion
1	can beef consommé soup	1½	cups long grain white rice, not
			instant

Melt margarine in casserole which has been sprayed with nonstick cooking spray. Pour in other ingredients and stir to combine. Cover with foil. Bake at 350 for 50 minutes. Uncover and bake an additional 10 minutes or until edges are brown.

Yield: 6-8 servings

Janet Carson Ricciarelli

Noodle and Rice Thang

1	cup converted rice	1	(4 ounce) can sliced
2	cups chicken broth		mushrooms, drained
1	(8 ounce) can sliced water	6	tablespoons butter
	chestnuts, drained	1	cup spaghetti noodles, broken
			into small pieces

Place rice, chicken broth, water chestnuts and mushrooms into a 2 quart casserole. In a medium sized skillet, melt butter. Add spaghetti. Brown. Stir spaghetti into the rice mixture. Cover and bake 40 minutes at 350.

Yield: 6-8 servings

Marti Mostellar

Baked Cheesy Noodles

¼	cup butter	2	cups milk
¼	cup chopped onions	1½	cups chopped processed cheese
¼	cup chopped celery		loaf
3	tablespoons flour	1	teaspoon prepared mustard
1	teaspoon salt	½	pound medium egg noodles

In a large skillet, melt butter. Add celery and onions. Sauté for about 10 minutes over medium heat. Sprinkle with flour and salt. Stir to blend. Cook and stir an additional 10 minutes over low heat. Remove from heat and cool 1 minute. Slowly add milk while stirring. Return to the medium heat and cook, stirring until mixture thickens. Add cheese and mustard. Cook noodles according to directions. Drain and stir into sauce. Place in a casserole and bake at 350 for 30 minutes or until browned on top.

Yield: 4 servings

Erma Auer

Pasta Alfredo

3	tablespoons butter	1	teaspoon pepper
1½	cups heavy whipping cream	½	teaspoon salt
¾	cup freshly grated Parmesan cheese	1	pound cooked pasta

In a medium saucepan, over medium low heat, melt butter. Add cream, salt and pepper. Stir in Parmesan cheese. Pour over cooked pasta. Serve with additional Parmesan cheese.

Yield: 6 servings

Louise Mauck

Stay at Home Pasta

5	cloves garlic, finely chopped	5	large tomatoes, chopped
2	medium Vidalia onions, chopped	½	cup fresh cilantro, chopped
	olive oil		salt and pepper to taste
5	green bell peppers, chopped	1	(16 ounce) package spaghetti noodles

Sauté garlic and onions in olive oil in a large skillet over medium heat. When onions are becoming transparent add green pepper. Cook for 2 minutes. Add remaining ingredients, except pasta. Cover and cook over medium heat for 5-10 minutes, stirring occasionally. Cook spaghetti according to directions. Toss with sauce.

Yield: 6 servings

Jane MacDonald

Tomato Basil Pasta

small box angel hair pasta
7-8 large cloves garlic, minced
2 tablespoons olive oil
juice of 1 lemon
3 teaspoons chopped fresh basil
¼ cup white wine

1 cup fresh diced tomatoes or
   canned diced tomatoes with
   green chilies
¾ small jar marinated artichoke
   hearts with juice, quartered

Prepare pasta according to package directions. Drain well and set aside. Sauté garlic in olive oil over low heat. Add lemon, basil, wine and tomatoes. Simmer on low heat about 10 minutes. Add artichoke hearts and small amount of juice to sauce. Stir well then toss with pasta. Serve immediately. If you like spicy hot pasta, add 1 teaspoon crushed red pepper to olive oil with garlic.

Yield: 4-6 servings

Dawn Davis

Zucchini Marinara

2 large zucchini, sliced
1 medium onion, peeled and diced
1 carrot, peeled and grated
2 (15 ounce) cans whole tomatoes,
   diced
1 (8 ounce) can tomato sauce

3 ounces tomato paste
1 tablespoon olive oil
1 teaspoon oregano
1 teaspoon seasoning salt
salt and pepper to taste

Place zucchini, onion and carrot in a medium sized pot. Add water to cover vegetables. Bring to a boil and cook until tender, approximately 10 minutes. Drain vegetables. Gently press out excess water from vegetables. Place them in a large pot. Add the remaining ingredients. Bring to a boil, reduce heat and simmer 30 minutes. Serve over spaghetti or angel hair pasta.

Yield: 4 servings

Shelia Hobgood

Sautéed Zucchini with Pink Tomato Sauce and Basil

2	tablespoons olive oil	½	teaspoon pepper
2	tablespoons butter	½	cup heavy cream
4	medium zucchini, sliced	1	cup shredded fresh basil
4	ripe tomatoes, cubed	1	pound penne pasta
2	cloves garlic, minced	¼	cup freshly grated Parmesan
1	teaspoon salt		cheese

In a medium skillet, heat oil and butter. Increase heat and without crowding, sauté zucchini until golden. Remove slices to a dish as they brown. Return browned zucchini to pan and add tomatoes, garlic, salt and pepper. Bring to a simmer. Add cream and simmer until thickened. Add basil. Cook pasta according to directions. Drain and toss with sauce. Top with Parmesan cheese.

Yield: 6 servings

Dina Trimboli Whitley, class of 80

Incredible Pimento Cheese

16	ounces cheddar cheese	½	teaspoon salt
16	ounces sharp cheddar cheese	½	teaspoon pepper
16	ounces processed cheese loaf	2	cups mayonnaise
3	tablespoons sugar	8	ounces diced pimento, drained

Shred cheese in a food processor using the grating blade. Using the steel blade, add sugar, salt, pepper and mayonnaise. Process to blend. Add pimento and pulse several times to blend.

Dina Trimboli Whitley, class of 80

Artichoke Frittata

1	tablespoon water	2	(6 ounce) jars marinated
½	pound fresh mushrooms, sliced		artichoke hearts, drained
1	cup chopped onions	1½	cups grated sharp cheddar
5	large eggs		cheese
1	(10 ounce) package chopped spinach, thawed and squeezed dry		

Butter a 1½ quart casserole. Place water, mushrooms and onions in a microwaveable bowl. Cover and cook on high 2-3 minutes. Beat eggs in a large bowl. Add mushroom mixture and all remaining ingredients. Bake covered 45 minutes at 350.

Yield: 6 servings

Debbie Gaskins

Fresh Vegetable Frittata

1	large sweet red pepper, chopped	7	large eggs, lightly beaten
1	cup sliced fresh mushrooms	½	cup mayonnaise
1½	cups shredded Swiss cheese	2	tablespoons chopped fresh basil
¼	pound asparagus, cut into 1 inch pieces		

Lightly grease a 9½ inch deep dish pie plate. Layer pepper, half the cheese and mushrooms in the pie pan. Top with asparagus and remaining cheese. Combine eggs and remaining ingredients. Pour evenly over cheese. Bake 55 minutes at 375. Let stand five minutes before serving.

Yield: 6 servings

Betty Lou Trimboli

Oven Omelet

¼	cup butter	2	cups shredded cheddar cheese
18	large eggs	1	(4 ounce) can sliced
1	cup sour cream		mushrooms, drained
1	cup milk	4	green onions, thinly sliced
2	teaspoons salt	1	(2 ounce) jar diced pimentos,
¼	teaspoon dried basil		drained

Melt butter in a 9x13 inch dish. Beat eggs, sour cream, milk, salt and basil to blend. Add remaining ingredients. Bake at 350 uncovered 45 minutes or until set.

Yield: 12 servings

Betty Lou Trimboli

Crustless Quiche

4	large eggs	2	cups shredded Swiss, Monterey
1	cup half and half		Jack and/or cheddar cheese
½	cup milk	2	tablespoons all purpose flour
½	teaspoon salt	1	cup chopped and sautéed
	dash cayenne pepper		mushrooms, peppers, ham or
			shrimp (optional)

Grease and flour a 9 inch round pan. (You may substitute a square pan for appetizer squares.) Mix eggs, half and half, milk, salt and pepper. Toss cheese with flour and place in prepared pan. Pour egg mixture over cheese. Bake at 350 for 40-45 minutes. Let stand 10 minutes before serving.

Yield: 6 main dish or 12 appetizer servings

Hint: Dip your sharp knife in warm water before slicing this quiche. Your slices will be neat.

Debbie Gaskins

Quiche for Kids

1	deep dish pie shell	2	cups shredded cheddar cheese
1½	cups milk	2	tablespoons flour
4	eggs	½	pound bacon, crisply cooked
½	teaspoon salt		and crumbled

Bake pie crust 5 minutes at 350. Remove from oven. In a medium bowl combine milk, eggs and salt. Mix well. Toss cheese with flour. Add cheese and bacon to the egg mixture. Pour into the pie crust. Bake at 350 for 40-45 minutes. Let stand 5 minutes before serving.

Yield: 6 servings

Sharon Hawkins

Two Easy Quiches

1	pound hot pork sausage	⅔	cup milk
1	cup shredded cheddar cheese or	1½	cups sour cream
	Swiss cheese	4	large eggs, beaten
1	cup shredded mozzarella or	½	teaspoon dry mustard
	Swiss cheese	2	(9 inch) pie crusts
1	teaspoon salt		

In a medium skillet, over medium heat, brown sausage. Drain and crumble. Divide evenly into the pie crusts and spread evenly in bottom of each pie crust. Divide the cheeses and spread over the sausage. In a medium bowl, mix the salt, milk, sour cream, eggs and mustard. Divide the milk mixture evenly into the pie crusts. Bake at 375 for 45-50 minutes. Let stand 10 minutes before serving.

Yield: 2 pies, 12-16 servings

Using this recipe, eat one quiche tonight and freeze the other for another night.

Jane Sylivant Newton, class of 87

My Quiche

½	pound sliced bacon	¼	teaspoon salt
¾	cup grated cheddar cheese	¼	teaspoon ground white pepper
¾	cup grated Swiss cheese		dash cayenne pepper
3	large eggs	1	(9 inch) deep dish pie shell,
1	cup milk		thawed
½	cup cream		

With kitchen shears, cut bacon into ½ inch pieces. Place in a microwaveable dish and cover with a paper towel. Microwave until crisp. Drain. Sprinkle evenly in pie crust. Sprinkle cheeses over bacon. In a medium sized bowl, mix together eggs, milk, cream, salt, pepper and cayenne pepper. Pour over the bacon and cheese. Bake at 375 for 45 minutes or until set. Let cool 10 minutes before serving.

Yield: 6-8 servings

Leraine Collier

Bacon and Cheese Quiche

½	pound bacon, cooked and crumbled	1	package dried onion soup mix
		½	cup milk
6	ounces Swiss cheese, grated	½	teaspoon salt
1	deep dish pie shell, thawed		dash of pepper, red pepper and
3	large eggs, beaten		nutmeg
6	ounces sour cream		pimento slices

In a medium sized bowl, mix together bacon and cheese. Spread into the bottom of pie shell. Blend the eggs, sour cream, dried soup mix, milk, salt, pepper, red pepper and nutmeg together in the bowl. Pour the mixture into the pie shell. Garnish with pimento. Bake at 350 for 30-40 minutes. Remove from oven and cool 10 minutes before serving.

Yield: 6-8 servings

Kathy White

89

Black Bean Pie

2	pie crusts	1	large jar salsa
2	(15 ounce) cans black beans, drained	2	cups shredded Monterey Jack cheese

Place one pie crust in a deep pie dish. Pour in the black beans. Top with the salsa then the cheese. Cover with the other pie crust. Pinch edges to seal. With a fork pierce the top crust several times. Bake at 350 for approximately 50 minutes or until crust browns.

Yield: 6 servings

Marti Mostellar

Robin and Olivia's Light and Easy Burritos

2	(15 ounce) cans fat-free refried beans	sliced jalapeño peppers, optional
1	(15 ounce) can kidney beans, drained	shredded cheddar cheese
1	(15 ounce) can salsa	flour tortillas
⅛	teaspoon cumin	low-fat sour cream
		shredded lettuce
		diced tomatoes

dash of hot sauce, optional

In a Dutch oven, mix refried beans, salsa, kidney beans, cumin, hot sauce and jalapeños, if desired. Bring to a boil. Simmer on low, stirring occasionally, until bean mixture begins to thicken. Spoon mixture into the center of tortilla. Sprinkle with cheese and fold "egg-roll" style. Place in a 9x13 inch baking dish and heat in 350 oven 5-10 minutes to melt cheese. Top with sour cream, lettuce and tomatoes. Serve immediately.

Yield: 8-12 servings

Omit the sour cream, lettuce and tomatoes and freeze the individual burritos.

Robert (Robin) Lee Wooten, class of 84

Black Beans and Rice

1	small package dried black beans (or 2-15 ounce cans black beans)	1	tablespoon dried parsley
		1	tablespoon seasoned salt substitute
3	(15 ounce) cans whole tomatoes, diced	1	teaspoon hot sauce
1	tablespoon dried onion		salt and pepper to taste
1	(6 ounce) can tomato paste		white or brown rice, cooked

Prepare beans according to package directions. When cooked, add all other ingredients, except rice. Bring to a boil, then reduce heat and simmer 30 minutes. Serve over rice.

8-10 servings

Shelia Hobgood

Bean Burritos

1	(16 ounce) can kidney beans, drained and mashed	1	teaspoon chili powder
			salt and pepper to taste
1	teaspoon dried cilantro	1	package whole wheat flour tortillas
1	teaspoon cumin		

Combine beans with all other ingredients, except tortillas. Cook 10 minutes. Wrap tortillas in foil and warm in 350 oven OR wrap tortillas in a warm towel and microwave 15 seconds. Place a scoop of bean mixture in the center of each tortilla and fold.

Yield: 4 servings

Joyce Witherington Mattux,
Sea Island Beach Club Spa, class of 77

Tomato and Goat Cheese Pizza

1	package canned biscuit dough	1	teaspoon dried oregano
5	large roma tomatoes, sliced	1	tablespoon dried basil
2	small red bell peppers, cut into strips	1	(15 ounce) can artichoke hearts, drained and chopped
1	clove garlic, minced	12	ounces goat cheese, crumbled
1	tablespoon minced onion		olive oil

Line baking sheet with parchment paper or use a nonstick baking sheet. Flatten each piece of biscuit dough into a four inch circle. Top each "pizza" with remaining ingredients. Drizzle each with olive oil and bake at 450 for 15 minutes.

Yield: 4-8 servings

Dina Trimboli Whitley, class of 80

Vegetable Pizza

1	package refrigerated crescent rolls	1	cup shredded lettuce
1	(8 ounce) package cream cheese	¼	cup chopped green pepper
½	cup salad dressing or mayonnaise	¼	cup shredded carrots
½	envelope ranch salad dressing	¼	cup chopped broccoli
		¼	cup chopped cauliflower
		¼	cup shredded cheddar cheese

Roll out the crescent rolls on a cookie sheet for crust. Cover the entire sheet with a thin layer of dough. Bake at 400 for 10 minutes. Cool. Mix cream cheese, salad dressing and ranch dressing packet. Spread on crust. Top with remaining ingredients in order listed. Cover with plastic wrap and refrigerate until ready to serve. Slice into wedges and serve.

Mini Pizzas

1   package English muffins
1   (8 ounce) can Italian style
    tomato sauce
1   pound bag shredded mozzarella
    cheese

assortment of toppings - olives,
sausage, pepperoni, peppers,
mushrooms, onions

Split muffins. Top each with sauce, then cheese. "Decorate" with your topping assortment. Place muffins on a baking sheet and bake at 400 for 3-4 minutes or until cheese is bubbly and melted.

Sarah Beth Blizzard

Rosemary Chicken with Penne Pasta

4   boneless chicken breasts
2   egg yolks
2½ cups half and half
1   cup grated Parmesan cheese
salt and pepper
12 ounces bacon

4   tablespoons butter
2   cloves garlic, crushed
3   teaspoons fresh rosemary leaves,
    minced
1   box penne pasta, prepared

Boil chicken until tender. Cut up and set aside. Whip egg yolks, cups half and half, Parmesan cheese, salt and pepper. Set aside. Cook bacon, reserving drippings. Set aside. Sauté garlic in butter and when lightly golden, remove and discard garlic. Add rosemary and cook for one minute. Add bacon and 6 tablespoons drippings. Blend well. Add chicken and mix. Remove from heat. Pour cream sauce over hot cooked pasta. Add bacon and chicken mixture to pasta. Mix well. Serve immediately.

Yield: 6 servings

Stephen Hill

Vegetarian Tacos

1	(15 ounce) can kidney beans	1	(8 ounce) package fat-free
1	package taco seasoning mix		cheese, shredded
6	taco shells, warmed	2	cups shredded lettuce
1	(8 ounce) container fat-free sour	2	medium tomatoes, cubed
	cream		

In a medium sized bowl, mash together kidney beans and seasoning mix. Fill taco shells with bean mixture. Top shells with sour cream, cheese, lettuce and tomatoes.

Yield: 6 servings

Joyce Witherington Mattux,
Sea Island Beach Club Spa, class of 77

Chicken Spaghetti

1	(4 pound) chicken	1	(28 ounce) can whole tomatoes,
7-8	cups water		chopped
1	tablespoon salt	½	cup sherry wine
½	cup chopped carrots	1½	cups chopped celery
½	cup chopped celery	1	(12 ounce) jar sliced mushrooms
½	cup chopped onions		salt, pepper and celery seeds to taste
1	large onion, chopped	1½	pounds spaghetti noodles

Place chicken in a large pot with water, salt, ½ cup carrots, ½ cup celery and ½ cup onions. Bring to a boil. Skim the gray waste. Cover and simmer at least one hour. Remove chicken. Cool and remove from bone. Strain the broth and return to pot. Sauté remaining onion and tomato. Add celery, sherry, mushrooms, salt, pepper and celery seeds. Add chicken and simmer. Cook spaghetti according to directions in the chicken broth. Top noodles with tomato sauce mixture.

Yield: 6-8 servings

Vegetarian Chili

4	onions, chopped	6	ounces tomato paste
1	green pepper, chopped	3	pounds red kidney beans
1	tablespoon olive oil		salt and pepper to taste
1	pound crushed tomatoes		

In bottom of a soup pot, over medium heat, sauté onion and green pepper in olive oil until tender. Add remaining ingredients. Simmer, covered for 40 minutes. Serve with crusty French bread and slaw.

Yield: 6 servings

Joyce Witherington Mattux,
Sea Island Beach Club Spa, class of 77

Chicken Tetrazzini

1	tablespoon oil	1	(15 ounce) can fat-free cream of mushroom soup
⅓	cup finely chopped celery		
⅓	cup finely chopped onion	1	(8 ounce) bag frozen peas, thawed
⅓	cup finely chopped bell pepper		
1	(4 ounce) can sliced mushrooms, drained	3	tablespoons Parmesan cheese
		2	cups grated cheddar cheese
1	(15 ounce) can chicken broth	2	cups cooked cutup chicken
		1	(8 ounce) box spaghetti, cooked

In a medium sized saucepan, heat the oil and add the celery, onion and bell pepper. Sauté until tender. Add the mushrooms, chicken broth, mushroom soup and peas. Gently blend in the chicken and pasta. Spread into two 9x13 inch ovenproof casserole pans. Top with cheeses. Bake at 325 for approximately 40 minutes or until bubbly.

Yield: 12 servings

If you are using leftover chicken and have leftover gravy as well, stir it into your sauce for added flavor.

Ginny Pollock

Chicken Tetrazzini

3 stalks celery, chopped	1 (8 ounce) package spaghetti,
1 onion, chopped	cooked in chicken stock
1 green pepper, chopped	8 ounces sharp cheese, grated
butter	6 ounce can mushrooms, drained
10-12 chicken breasts, boiled and	reserved chicken stock
deboned, reserve stock	

Sauté celery, onion and green pepper in butter. Layer in buttered casserole: chicken, spaghetti, sautéed items, cheese and mushrooms. Fill casserole half full with chicken stock. Bake at 350 for 25-30 minutes.

Ella Rodgman

Chicken and Wild Rice Casserole

3 small or 2 large chicken breasts	1 can cream of mushroom soup
1 onion, diced	1 (8 ounce) container sour cream
1 celery stalk, diced	1 (2 ounce) jar diced pimentos
1 carrot, diced	1 (4 ounce) can water chestnuts,
dash of salt	sliced
1 (6 ounce) package of long grain	1 small jar mushrooms
wild rice	1 cup grated cheese

Cook chicken with onion, celery, carrot and salt. Remove from bone and cut into small pieces. Reserve broth. Cook rice in reserved stock following directions on rice package, but using 2¼ cups stock. Combine all ingredients except cheese. Pour into lightly buttered 2 quart casserole dish. Top with cheese and bake at 325 for 30 minutes or until bubbly.

Yield: 6-8 servings

You may substitute ingredients with fat-free ingredients. Whole chicken or turkey pieces may be used in lieu of chicken breasts.

Kathy Sawyer

Italian Chicken and Rice

4 chicken breast halves, skinned and boned	½ cup water
½ teaspoon salt	1 cup long grain rice, uncooked
2 tablespoons margarine	¼ cup grated Parmesan cheese
½ cup chopped onion	½ teaspoon Italian seasoning
1 can Italian stewed tomatoes	¼ teaspoon garlic powder
1 (13¾ ounce) can chicken broth	4 ounces mozzarella cheese, cut into ¼ inch slices

Season chicken breasts with salt. In a large skillet, over medium heat, melt margarine. Add chicken, cooking until browned. Combine remaining ingredients, except mozzarella cheese, and pour into a casserole dish. Top with browned chicken breasts. Cover and bake at 350 for 45-50 minutes. Uncover dish and top with mozzarella cheese. Bake an additional 15 minutes.

Yield: 4 servings

Can be prepared early in the day and reheated.

Lynda Blount

Creole Jambalaya

2 tablespoons butter	3 cups chicken broth
1 pound kielbasa, chopped or sliced	1 bay leaf, crushed
2 large onions, chopped with 2 garlic cloves	½ teaspoon thyme
	½ teaspoon chili powder
1 medium green pepper, cut up	¼ teaspoon pepper
4⅔ cups tomatoes (2 pound 3 ounce cans)	2 cups long grain rice
	1 pound shrimp, peeled and deveined

Melt butter in large casserole or Dutch oven. Add sausage, onion and garlic. Cook until lightly browned. Add remaining ingredients except rice and shrimp. Bring to a boil. Gradually stir in rice. Cover and simmer for 30 minutes or until rice is tender and liquid is absorbed. Add shrimp and more seasonings if desired. Continue cooking until shrimp is done. You can vary amounts of sausage and shrimp.

Yield: 6-8 servings

Evelyn Deane

Red Beans and Rice

2	tablespoons vegetable or olive oil or 1 tablespoon bacon drippings and 1 tablespoon oil	2	(15 ounce) cans dark red kidney beans, not drained
1	tablespoon flour	1	cup stale beer or ½ cup red wine and ½ cup water
1	cup chopped onions	½	teaspoon hot sauce
½	cup chopped green pepper, optional		salt and pepper to taste
½	cup chopped celery, optional	1-2	cups sliced smoked sausage or ½ sausage and ½ ham
		2	cups cooked rice

In a large heavy frying pan, over medium high heat, add the oil and stir in flour. Reduce heat and stir constantly for 10-15 minutes or until golden brown. Add chopped onions, green pepper and celery. Stir over medium heat for 5-10 minutes. Pour in beans and bean juice. Stir to blend. Add the beer or wine/water mixture, a little at a time, stirring to blend until you reach a thick soupy consistency. Add salt, pepper and hot sauce. Reduce heat to low and cover. In a heavy skillet, over medium heat, cook the sausage for approximately 8 minutes or until the sausage is browning. Add the sausage and drippings to the bean mixture. Add the ham, if desired. Cook covered, over low heat, for 40 minutes. Serve over rice.

Yield: 6 servings

Vicki Hallberg

Hamburger Casserole

1	tablespoon oil	½	teaspoon garlic salt
1	pound lean ground beef	¼	teaspoon chili powder
1	medium onion, chopped	1	cup cooked rice
1	green pepper, chopped	1	(15 ounce) can corn, drained
1	(15 ounce) can chopped tomatoes	½	cup grated cheddar cheese
			paprika

In a large skillet, over medium high heat, brown beef, onion and pepper in oil. Drain. Add tomatoes, garlic salt and chili powder. Simmer for 15 minutes. Add rice and corn and stir to blend. Pour mixture into a two quart ovenproof casserole. Top with cheese. Sprinkle with paprika and bake at 350 for 30 minutes or until bubbly.

Yield: 6 servings

Jennifer Heath Sutton, class of 90

Kielbasa Kabobs with Red Beans and Rice

2   pounds kielbasa, sliced into two   inch pieces
1   large onion, cut into eighths
1   large bell pepper, cut into eighths
1   (14 ounce) jar picante sauce
2   (8 ounce) bags Cajun red beans   and rice, cooked

Preheat grill. Into a large pot of water, put kielbasa, onion and pepper. Bring to a boil over high heat. Drain. Run cold water over to cool completely. Skewer, alternating kielbasa, onions and peppers, ending with kielbasa. Grill prepared skewers, turning frequently for 5-10 minutes or until sausages are browned. Serve over prepared rice and top with picante sauce.

Yield: 4 servings

Jo Allen, class of 76

Cherokee Casserole

1   pound lean ground beef
¼   cup chopped onions
salt and pepper to taste
1⅛ teaspoons dried garlic
⅛   teaspoon oregano
1   cup cooked rice
1   (8 ounce) can cream of   mushroom soup
1   (8 ounce) can diced tomatoes,   drained
2   cups shredded cheddar cheese

In a large skillet, over medium high heat, brown the onions and the beef. Drain fat. Stir in salt, pepper, garlic and oregano. Add rice, soup and tomatoes. Stir to blend. Bring to a simmer and cook for 10 minutes, covered. Remove the cover and sprinkle with cheese. Replace lid and simmer an additional 5-10 minutes.

Yield: 6 servings

Pam Cunningham

Quick Southern Red Beans and Rice

1 bag dried red kidney beans, washed	1 large bell pepper, seeded and cut in half
water	3 tablespoons (or to taste) Cajun seasoning with salt
2 packages smoked sausage	2 cups long grain rice
1 large onion, scored on ends	4 cups water
3 stalks celery, each cut in half	2 teaspoons salt

In large pot, place dried beans. Add enough water to cover beans under 3-4 inches water. Cook on high heat until boiling and beans begin to float to top. Remove from heat, cover and let sit for 15 minutes. Cut smoked sausage into ¼ inch slices. Add to beans. Add onion, celery, bell pepper and Cajun seasoning. Cover and cook over medium low heat for one hour. Remove wilted onion, celery and bell pepper. Discard. With slotted spoon, remove from pot approximately 2 tablespoons beans. Mash with the back of spoon and return to pot, stirring constantly to thicken. Boil 4 cups water. Add rice and salt. Cover and lower heat to simmer for 20 minutes or until water is absorbed. Serve beans and sausage over rice. Serve with catsup and hot sauce. For more flavor, one stick of margarine or butter may be added to beans when adding sausage. Smoked ham bones also add great flavor without the added fat. Leftover smoked ham may be used in place of or in addition to the sausage. Serve with corn bread muffins. Great for those picky eaters who don't care for chunks of onion or celery in their food.

Yield: 8-10 servings

Susan King

So Easy Taco Rice with Cheese Quesadillas

1	pound ground beef	2	cups water
1	package taco seasoning mix	2	(8 ounce) packages shredded
8	ounces mild taco sauce or salsa		cheddar cheese
1	cup rice, uncooked	1	package flour tortillas
			nonstick cooking spray

In skillet, brown beef. Add taco seasoning, taco sauce or salsa, rice and water. Simmer, covered, 20 minutes or until water is absorbed. Remove from heat. Top with 8 ounces cheese and replace lid until cheese melts. To make quesadillas, spray one side of each tortilla with nonstick cooking spray. Place sprayed side down onto hot griddle. Top with approximately ¼ cup cheese then with another tortilla, sprayed side up. Fry 1-2 minutes on each side, until lightly browned. Using kitchen shears, cut each quesadilla into six or eight wedges, pizza style. Serve hot. If desired, shredded lettuce, tomatoes, black olives, sour cream and additional taco sauce may be served on the side. I've never had a finicky nose turned up at this! Fast and easy!

Yield: 4-6 servings

Susan King

Spaghetti Stroganoff

	stew beef, cut into small pieces	2	cans tomato soup
1	small onion, diced	1	dash hot pepper sauce
3	tablespoons oil	1½	tablespoons Worcestershire sauce
	minced garlic	1	small carton sour cream
1	small can chopped mushrooms, drained		spaghetti noodles, prepared according to package directions

Fry chopped stew beef with onion in oil until done. Drain. Add garlic, mushrooms, soup, hot pepper sauce and Worcestershire sauce. Simmer 45 minutes. Add sour cream and mix well. Serve over spaghetti.

Yield: 4-6 servings

Sharon Seawell

Spaghetti Casserole

1   pound hamburger
1   large can crushed tomatoes
1   (12 ounce) can tomato sauce
1   onion, chopped
1   small jar mushrooms, optional
1   package spaghetti sauce
     seasoning mix
¼   cup brown sugar
salt to taste
1   tablespoon minced garlic
fresh basil
1   pound spaghetti or other pasta,
     cooked

Brown hamburger, drain and add all ingredients, except pasta. Simmer on low to medium low for 2 hours. Cover the bottom of a 3 quart baking dish with sauce. Add pasta. Cover with remaining sauce and cheese. Bake at 350 for 20 minutes. Serve with salad and garlic bread. Use the prepared Caesar salad found in the produce section of the grocery store and toss with bottled Caesar dressing.

Kim Stokes

Crescent Lasagna

½   pound sausage
½   pound ground beef
¾   cup chopped onions
½   clove garlic, minced
1   tablespoon dried parsley
½   teaspoon dried oregano
½   teaspoon basil
½   teaspoon salt
2   (6 ounce) cans tomato paste
1   cup cottage cheese
1   egg
¼   cup grated Parmesan cheese
2   cups shredded mozzarella cheese
2   cans refrigerator crescent rolls

Brown sausage and ground beef. Add onions, garlic, parsley, oregano, basil salt, pepper and tomato paste. Set aside. Mix together cottage cheese, egg and Parmesan cheese. Set aside. On a cookie sheet or jelly roll pan, form one large crust with the crescent rolls to make a rectangular shaped crust, pressing edges together. Layer meat and cheese mixtures down the center of crust. Top with mozzarella cheese. Fold sides and ends of pastry over filling to completely enwrap filling. Bake at 375 for 20-25 minutes or until browned. May be prepared ahead and refrigerated for 2-3 hours before baking.

Yield: 6-8 servings

For added flavor, brush top with milk then sprinkle with sesame seeds.

Sharlene Vainright

Ham, Peas and Bowties

2	tablespoons oil	1	(10 ounce) package frozen peas,
1	medium onion, diced		thawed
2	cups sliced mushrooms	½	cup chicken broth
2	cloves garlic, minced	2	tablespoons lemon juice
2	cups cubed ham	1	(16 ounce) package bowtie pasta
		½	cup grated Parmesan cheese

In a large skillet, heat oil over medium heat. Add onion, mushrooms and garlic. Cook, stirring, for 3 minutes. Stir in ham, peas, chicken broth and lemon juice. Over high heat, cook for several minutes, stirring, until half the liquid has evaporated. Cook pasta according to directions. Pour mixture over pasta. Add Parmesan cheese and toss to mix thoroughly. Serve with additional cheese.

Yield: 6 servings

Stephanie Hill

Spaghetti Carbonara

1	pound bacon	½	cup chopped fresh parsley
3	eggs, beaten		salt and pepper to taste
⅓	cup heavy cream	1	(16 ounce) box linguine
1	cup grated Parmesan cheese		

With kitchen shears, cut bacon into ½ inch pieces. Place in a microwaveable dish and microwave until crisp, stirring to separate. Remove to a paper towel to drain. Pour heavy cream into a microwaveable measuring cup and heat in microwave until warm to the touch. Blend in salt, pepper and eggs. Cook the pasta al dente. Drain. Quickly toss the pasta with the cream mixture to coat. Add bacon, parsley and cheese. Add a tablespoon bacon drippings if it seems too dry.

Yield: 5-6 servings

Leftover ham is a good substitute for the bacon.

Cathy Green

Shrimp and Spanish Rice

1	pound fresh shrimp, peeled and deveined	1	(14½ ounce) can chopped tomatoes
margarine		⅓	cup diced green pepper
1	package Spanish Rice	½	cup diced celery

Sauté shrimp in margarine. Set aside. Sauté green pepper and celery until slightly tender. Set aside. Prepare rice according to package directions. When rice is done, add shrimp, green pepper and celery to rice mixture. Heat for 5-10 minutes. Serve immediately.

Yield: 4 servings

Bonnie Everette

Daddy Pat's Pasta

2	sticks butter	8	ounces angel hair pasta
6	cloves garlic, finely minced	1	cup marinated sun-dried tomatoes, chopped or ½ cup sun-dried tomato bits
1	pound scallops or peeled shrimp		
2	cups finely chopped parsley	½	cup freshly grated Parmesan cheese
freshly ground pepper			
salt to taste			

In large skillet, over medium heat, melt butter. Add garlic and sauté. Add scallops or shrimp and sauté. Stir in parsley, pepper and salt. Cook pasta according to directions. Drain and place in a shallow bowl. Pour sauce over pasta and gently toss to coat. Sprinkle with sun-dried tomatoes and Parmesan cheese.

Yield: 5-6 servings

Sun-dried tomatoes come packaged many ways, in bits, oil or dried. The dried must be reconstituted before using.

Marty Patterson Chapman, class of 76

Light Fettuccini with Shrimp

1½ tablespoons light butter
1   teaspoon finely chopped garlic
1   teaspoon onion salt
2   tablespoons flour
1½ cups gourmet fat-free half and half
1   pound shrimp, cooked, peeled and deveined

12 ounces fettuccini
2   tablespoons chopped fresh parsley
½   cup freshly grated Parmesan cheese or fat-free Parmesan cheese
    freshly ground black pepper

In a medium skillet, melt butter and sauté garlic. Remove from heat and add onion salt and flour. Stir to blend flour thoroughly. Heat until bubbly, approximately 1-2 minutes. Don't allow the flour to brown. Remove from heat and let cool briefly. Whisk in half and half. Return to medium heat, whisk constantly until mixture boils and thickens. Add shrimp and simmer 3-5 minutes. Cook pasta according to directions. Drain and toss with sauce. Sprinkle with parsley, cheese and pepper

Yield: 6 servings

Tena Hardee

Tuna Casserole

2   cans tuna, drained
1   can cream of mushroom soup
1   tablespoon Worcestershire sauce

8   ounces elbow macaroni, cooked and drained
    potato chips

Combine first four ingredients. Pack into greased casserole dish. Cover with broken chips. Bake at 325 for 15-20 minutes.

Sandra Warren

Linguine Mediterranean

6	slices bacon, cut into 1 inch pieces	½	cup minced fresh parsley
1	medium onion, diced	½-1	teaspoon crushed red pepper
½	pound fresh mushrooms, sliced		salt and pepper to taste
1	(10 ounce) can whole baby clams, broth included	1	pound linguine
		¼	cup butter
			freshly grated Parmesan cheese

In a medium sized skillet, cook bacon until crisp. Drain on paper towels. Reserve 1 tablespoon drippings. Add onion to the reserved drippings and sauté until soft. Stir in mushrooms, clams and broth. Cook over moderate heat for 10 minutes, stirring occasionally. Add parsley, bacon, red pepper, salt and pepper. Stir. Cook linguine according to directions. Drain and toss with butter. Pour sauce over pasta and serve with Parmesan.

Yield: 4-5 servings

Penny Pelletier Manning, class of 84

Chicken

JIM
OSTROWSKI

Apricot Chicken

1 cup apricot preserves	1 onion, sliced or 1 package dry
1 cup fat-free Russian or Catalina	onion soup mix
dressing	6 boneless, skinless chicken breasts

Mix first three ingredients. Place chicken in baking dish. Cover with sauce. Microwave 15 minutes on high. Broil to brown chicken to liking, or you may bake at 375 for 40 minutes. Serve with rice and steamed broccoli. Sprinkle broccoli with butter or lemon juice.

Joyce Witherington Mattux,
Sea Island Beach Club Spa, class of 77

Cheddar Cheese Chicken

2 tablespoons butter or margarine	1 can cheddar cheese soup
2 pounds chicken parts or breasts	water
only	

Melt butter in ovenproof dish in 400 oven. Add chicken to dish and return to oven. Bake 20 minutes. Turn and bake an additional 20 minutes. In a small bowl, combine soup and a small amount of water to obtain a creamy consistency. Pour over chicken. Bake an additional 20 minutes.

Yield: 4-6 servings

Hudoch Family

Chicken Bundles

chicken breasts (one per bundle)	1 tablespoon butter or margarine
diced carrots to taste	per bundle
diced or sliced potatoes to taste	1 tablespoon white cooking sherry
1 slice onion per bundle	or white wine per bundle
1 slice green bell pepper per bundle	dash lemon juice per bundle

Using heavy duty foil, place one chicken breast in center of foil and add other ingredients. Close foil around bundle. Bake at 350 for 1½ hours or grill.

Carla Lancaster

Balsamic Chicken Breasts

4	boneless, skinless chicken breasts	½	cup chicken broth
½	teaspoon salt	3	tablespoons balsamic vinegar
¼	teaspoon pepper	1	teaspoon brown sugar
1	tablespoon olive oil	1	tablespoon butter
¼	cup minced shallots		

Sprinkle chicken with salt and pepper. Cook in oil over medium heat. Remove and add shallots. Cook two minutes. Add broth, vinegar and brown sugar. Boil and reduce by ⅓. Whisk in butter. Add chicken. Serve with pasta.

Yield: 4 servings

Dina Trimboli Whitley, class of 80

Breezy Barbecued Chicken

1	cup salad oil	1	teaspoon dry mustard
⅓	cup white vinegar	1	tablespoon Worcestershire sauce
3	tablespoons sugar	1	clove garlic, minced
3	tablespoons catsup		dash hot sauce
1	tablespoon grated onion	3	(2 pound) broiler chickens,
1½	teaspoons salt		halved

Combine first 10 ingredients and mix well. Add chicken and marinate in refrigerator overnight. Grill chicken over medium heat about 45 minutes turning and basting with marinade.

Yield: 6 servings

Ella Rodgman

Chicken and Asparagus Casserole

2	chicken breasts, skinned, deboned and cut into 2x4 inch pieces	2	(10 ounce) packages frozen asparagus, or two cans
1½	teaspoons tenderizing salt	1	can cream of chicken soup
¼	teaspoon pepper	½	cup mayonnaise
½	cup oil	1	teaspoon lemon juice
		½	teaspoon curry powder
		1	cup grated sharp cheese

Sprinkle tenderizing salt and pepper over chicken and sauté in oil over medium heat for about six minutes or until chicken is white. Drain well on paper towels. Cook asparagus. Drain well. Place asparagus in bottom of 9x13 inch casserole. Place chicken over asparagus. Mix soup, mayonnaise, lemon juice and curry powder. Pour over chicken. Sprinkle cheese on top and cover. Bake at 375 for 30-40 minutes.

Ella Rodgman

Chicken Cordon Bleu

6	chicken breast halves, boneless	2	tablespoons grated Parmesan cheese
	salt and pepper		
6	thin slices of ham	2	tablespoons minced parsley
3	slices Swiss cheese, halved	¼	cup margarine, melted
½	cup round cracker crumbs		

Place breast on cutting board. Cover with wax paper and pound to flatten. Lightly salt and pepper. Place slice of ham and slice of cheese on each breast. Roll breast jelly roll style and secure with toothpick. Combine cracker crumbs, Parmesan cheese and parsley. Dip breast in margarine, then crumb mixture. Place in greased casserole dish and bake at 350 for 45 minutes.

Yield: 6 servings

Vickie Waters Downing, class of 80

Chicken Celebre

3-4 pounds chicken thighs or breasts skinned	2 packages dry onion soup mix
1 bottle Italian dressing	2 cans mushroom caps, drained
1 teaspoon oregano	4-6 tomatoes, quartered
	2 bay leaves

Place chicken in 9x13 dish. Mix dressing, oregano and soup mix in bowl. Spoon over chicken. Arrange mushroom caps and tomatoes around chicken. Place bay leaves on top. Bake at 350 for 1½ hours. I put ½ cup water around chicken so that it will not dry out. I also cover it with foil the first hour and remove it for the last 30 minutes for browning. Serve with wild rice. This is a Virginia dish. It's easy and delicious. Great for Thanksgiving or anytime a whole turkey is too much. Great for company.

Anita Watson

Cream of Chicken and Mushrooms

3 pounds chicken	1 teaspoon dried thyme
chopped onions and bay leaf	1 teaspoon salt
1½ sticks butter	1 teaspoon garlic
¾ cup minced onion	1 cup flour
½ cup minced celery	5 cups (or more) chicken broth
4 cups sliced mushrooms	2¼ cups cream

Precook chicken with bay leaf and chopped onions. Strain liquid and use for chicken broth. Melt butter and sauté minced onions, mushrooms and celery. Add thyme, salt and garlic. Sauté until onion is clear. Add flour to make roux. Cook this mixture on moderate heat 3 5 minutes. May add some broth if too thick. Add chicken, then broth slowly while stirring. Cook for 5 minutes on moderate heat, stirring constantly. Add cream to soup mixture. Serve immediately.

Yield: 6-8 servings

Samia Garner

Chicken and Ham Roll-ups

3   whole chicken breasts, split,
     skinned and deboned
6   slices boiled ham
2   tablespoons butter or margarine

1   can cream of chicken soup
¼   cup Chablis or other dry white
     wine

Place chicken between two sheets of waxed paper. Flatten with the flat side of a knife. Top each breast with a slice of ham. Roll up and secure with toothpicks. Brown in butter or margarine. Stir in soup and wine. Cover and cook over low heat for 20 minutes or until done. Stir occasionally.

Yield: 6 servings

Laura Hobbs Lutz, class of 75

Crunchy Chicken Imperial

½   pint sour cream
2   tablespoons lemon juice
2   teaspoons Worcestershire sauce
1   teaspoon celery salt
1   teaspoon paprika
½   teaspoon salt

½   teaspoon pepper
8   chicken breasts, deboned and
     skinned
1   package crushed herb-seasoned
     stuffing mix
½   cup butter, melted

Mix first seven ingredients. Place mixture and chicken breasts in a zip-top plastic bag and refrigerate 6-8 hours or overnight. Remove chicken breast and roll in crushed stuffing mix. Spray baking dish with nonstick cooking spray and place rolled chicken breasts in dish. Pour or brush melted butter on chicken. Bake at 350, uncovered, for 1-1½ hours. If chicken browns too quickly, cover lightly with foil for the last 20 minutes.

Yield: 8 servings

Betty Andrews

Low-Fat Chicken Breasts with Sherried Mushrooms

1¼ cups nonfat chicken broth, undiluted
2 tablespoons flour
¼ teaspoon salt
¼ teaspoon pepper
4 (4 ounce) skinned, boned chicken breast halves
nonstick cooking spray
1 tablespoon reduced calorie margarine
2 cups sliced fresh mushrooms
½ cup sliced green onions
4 tablespoons dry sherry, divided
1½ teaspoons cornstarch
1 tablespoon chopped fresh parsley

Place chicken broth in small saucepan. Bring to a boil. Set aside. Combine flour, salt and pepper. Sprinkle over chicken. Coat a non-stick skillet with nonstick spray. Over medium high heat, cook chicken 5 minutes on each side until browned. Remove. Clean skillet. Again, spray skillet. Add margarine and melt. Add mushrooms and green onions. Sauté until tender. Combine 1 tablespoon sherry and cornstarch. Stir well. Set aside. Add remaining 3 tablespoons sherry and broth to skillet. Bring to boil. Add cornstarch mixture and cook about one minute or until thickened. Return chicken to skillet. Cover. Reduce heat and simmer 10 minutes or until heated thoroughly. Transfer chicken to platter. Top with mushroom mixture, sprinkle with parsley.

Yield: 4 servings (5.6 g. fat, 197 calories)

Ada Nunn

Chicken Diablo

1 can cream of mushroom soup
¾ cup salsa
¼ teaspoon cumin
6 boneless skinless chicken breasts
1 (14 ounce) can artichoke hearts, quartered

Mix soup, salsa and cumin. Put chicken in baking dish. Bake at 350 for 20 minutes. Place artichoke hearts around chicken. Pour soup over top. Bake an additional 30 minutes or until chicken is done.

Dina Trimboli Whitley, class of 80

Chicken Piccata

1	egg	⅛	teaspoon garlic powder
3	tablespoons lemon juice	¼	cup margarine
4	boneless, skinless chicken breasts, pounded	2	teaspoons chicken bouillon granules
¼	cup all purpose flour	½	cup water

Mix egg and 1 tablespoon lemon juice. Combine flour and garlic powder. Dip chicken in lemon and egg mixture and dredge in flour and garlic mixture. Brown in margarine. Add bouillon, water and 2 tablespoons lemon juice. Simmer covered for 20 minutes. Sauce may be doubled if desired.

Yield: 4 servings

Lisa Hines

Marinated Chicken Breasts

6	boneless, skinless chicken breasts	3	tablespoons mustard
½	cup firmly packed brown sugar	1½	tablespoons lemon juice
⅓	cup olive oil	1½	tablespoons lime juice
¼	cup cider vinegar	1½	teaspoons salt
3	cloves garlic, crushed	¼	teaspoon pepper

Place chicken breasts in large shallow dish. Combine remaining ingredients. Stir well. Pour over chicken. Cover and refrigerate overnight. The longer it marinates, the better. Remove chicken from marinade and grill over hot coals about 8 minutes on each side. Serve as an entrée or on a sandwich roll with lettuce and tomato.

Yield: 6 servings

Kathy White

Lemon Chicken

¼ cup lemon juice
½ cup margarine or butter, melted
1   teaspoon garlic powder
1   teaspoon poultry seasoning

½ teaspoon salt
¼ teaspoon pepper
4   boneless, skinless chicken breasts

Combine all ingredients, except chicken. Pour over chicken in oven-proof baking dish. Bake uncovered at 350 for 45 minutes to 1 hour, basting frequently. To complete this meal, serve with white rice, steamed vegetables and hot rolls.

Yield: 4 servings

Debi Lee

Shortcut Chicken Pot Pie

1   package skinless, boneless
    chicken breasts
1   package frozen broccoli,
    cauliflower and carrots
2   cans healthy variety cream of
    chicken soup

2   small cans no salt added mixed
    vegetables
1   cup chicken broth
1   can sliced water chestnuts
1   can green peas, drained
1   can refrigerator breadsticks

Steam chicken breasts and cut into small pieces. Cook frozen vegetables in broth 5 minutes. Mix all ingredients, except breadsticks, and place in greased casserole. Lay bread sticks, lattice-style, on top for crust. Bake at 350 for 1 hour.

Lee Adams

Sweet and Sour Chicken

2   boneless and skinless chicken   2   jars prepared sweet and sour
    breasts   sauce
                                            prepared rice

Boil chicken breasts until tender. Cut into small pieces and put in pan. Pour jars of sweet and sour sauce over chicken and let it simmer for 15 minutes. Serve over rice.

Yield: 4 servings

Jennifer Heath Sutton, class of 90

Chicken Casserole

2   cups chicken, cooked   1   cup mayonnaise
2   cups chopped celery   1   small can pineapple tidbits
½   cup slivered almonds   1   small can green peas
½   teaspoon salt   ½   cup grated American cheese
2   teaspoons grated onion   ½   cup crushed potato chips
2   teaspoons lemon juice

Toss first 9 ingredients together. Place in casserole dish. Top with cheese and potato chips. Bake at 425 for 15-20 minutes.

Ella Rodgman

Chicken Divan

2   packages frozen broccoli   1   cup grated sharp cheddar cheese
4   chicken breasts, cooked and   ½   cup water
    sliced   ¾   cup crushed crackers
1   can cream of mushroom soup

Cook and drain broccoli. Lay in 9x13 inch greased pan. Place sliced chicken breasts on top. Combine soup, cheese and water. Spread over chicken. Sprinkle crackers on top and bake at 350 for 30 minutes. Serve with wild rice or other flavored rice and fruit salad.

Yield: 4 servings

Kathy White

Walnut Cheese Chicken Breasts

¾ cup part-skim ricotta cheese
½ cup finely chopped walnuts
¼ cup grated Parmesan cheese
2   tablespoons fresh breadcrumbs
salt and pepper to taste
½ tablespoon fresh parsley

1½ tablespoons fresh basil
4   chicken breast halves with skin
     and bones
olive oil
¼ cup dry white wine

Lightly oil a baking dish large enough to hold chicken. Combine ricotta cheese, walnuts, Parmesan cheese, bread crumbs, salt and pepper. Slip fingers gently between skin and meat of chicken breast and stuff ¼ of cheese filling under skin. Repeat with remaining chicken breasts. Place chicken in baking dish and brush with olive oil. Sprinkle with wine and season with salt and pepper. Bake chicken at 375 for 35-40 minutes, basting occasionally.

Yield: 4 servings

Linda Peacock

Cajun Chicken

¼ cup margarine
2   tablespoons all purpose flour
1   cup milk
1   pound chicken breasts, cut into
     thin strips
½ teaspoon tarragon leaves
1   cup hot cooked peas

1   (2 ounce) jar diced pimentos,
     drained
1   bag instant rice, cooked
Cajun spice blend which is ¼
     teaspoon each of: black pepper,
     white pepper, red pepper, garlic
     powder, paprika, salt

In a small saucepan, over medium-low heat, melt 2 tablespoons margarine. Stir in flour, cook for 2 minutes. Slowly add milk and ¾ teaspoon spice blend. Cook, stirring constantly until thickened. Keep warm. In a skillet, over medium-high heat, melt remaining margarine. Add chicken, tarragon and remaining spice blend. Sauté until chicken is done. Keep warm. Gently stir together peas, pimentos and rice. Spoon chicken mixture over rice mixture. Serve with prepared sauce.

Anita Watson

Chicken and Dumplings

1½ cups chopped onions
1 tablespoon butter
olive oil
1 chicken, cut up or 4-6 breasts
salt and pepper to taste

2 cups water
2 chicken bouillon cubes, optional
1½ cups chopped carrots or the
   small ready to eat kind
1 cup chopped celery

Dumplings:
1½ cups flour
4 teaspoons baking powder
½ teaspoon salt
½ teaspoon nutmeg

1 tablespoon shortening
1 egg, well beaten
⅔ cup milk

In iron pot or skillet with a good fitting lid, sauté onions in butter and several tablespoons olive oil for about 10 minutes or until golden. Sear the chicken on both sides until golden. Add salt, pepper, water, bouillon, carrots and celery. Cover and simmer about 1 hour. Remove chicken and bring to full boil, adding more liquid. You need enough to almost cover dumplings. Mix up dumplings and drop small egg size lumps of dough into boiling broth. Cover and cook for 15 minutes.

Judy Johnson

Chicken Pockets

1 package of 8 crescent rolls
2 cups chicken, cooked and cut
   into chunks
3 ounces cream cheese

2 tablespoons milk
2 tablespoons pimentos
chives, for taste and color
salt and pepper to taste

Spread crescent rolls to make four squares. Mix together remaining ingredients and place ½ cup mixture in each square. Fold corners over mixture. Press seams of crescent rolls tightly to prevent excessive draining when baking. Bake at 325 for 30 minutes or until rolls are golden. Great for festive family holiday meal — easy and colorful.

Yield: 4 servings

Lisa Britt Carrigan, class of 81

Chicken Pizza

pizza crust
2   boneless, skinless chicken breasts
    cut into small pieces
ranch dressing

taco seasoning
bacon bits
Monterey Jack and cheddar cheese

Spread ranch dressing over pizza crust. Sauté chicken and sprinkle with taco seasoning. Place chicken on pizza crust. Cover with cheeses. I sometimes add caramelized onions and sautéed peppers. Bake at 425 for 12-15 minutes.

Yield: 2 servings

Kay Gross

Carole's Chicken Enchiladas

4   large chicken breasts with rib
    meat
½   teaspoon garlic salt
1   teaspoon salt
½   teaspoon pepper
⅓   cup sour cream
1   (4 ounce) can green chilies
1   teaspoon cumin

onion salt to taste
3   cups cheddar and/or Monterey
    Jack cheese
1   package (or can) enchilada
    sauce mix
½   cup peanut oil
16 corn tortillas

Bring chicken, garlic salt, salt and pepper to a boil. Reduce to medium-low. Cover and simmer 30 minutes. Remove chicken from broth and cool. Reserve broth for another use. Shred chicken with fingers. Should equal approximately 2½ cups. Add sour cream, chilies, cumin and onion salt. Cover and set aside. Prepare enchilada sauce according to package directions. Keep warm. Heat oil in skillet until hot and fry each tortilla a few seconds on each side to soften. Drain on paper towels, patting to remove excess oil. Place 1 cup enchilada sauce in a large glass baking dish. Divide 2 cups of the cheese into 16 parts. Divide chicken mixture likewise. Place chicken and cheese on each tortilla and roll up, placing seam down into sauce in dish. Cover with remaining sauce. (I don't always use all that is left, it may be too much and could cause enchiladas to be soggy.) Top with remaining 1 cup cheese. Bake at 350 for 20-30 minutes until hot and bubbly. Good served with tossed salad and Mexican Rice.

Yield: 6-8 servings

Carole Cameron

Oven-Fried Chicken Chimichangas

3   (5 ounce) cans white chicken,
    drained and flaked
1   (4 ounce) can chopped green
    chilies, drained

1   cup shredded Monterey Jack
    cheese
½   cup chopped green onions
8   (9 inch) flour tortillas
    vegetable oil

Combine first four ingredients and set aside. Wrap tortillas in damp paper towels and microwave on high 15 seconds or until hot. Brush both sides of tortillas with vegetable oil. Keep warm. Place a scant ½ cup chicken mixture just below center of each tortilla. Fold in left and right sides of tortilla to partially enclose filling. Fold up bottom edge of tortilla. Fold into a rectangle and secure with a wooden toothpick. Repeat with remaining tortillas and chicken mixture. Place filled tortillas on a lightly greased baking sheet. Bake at 425 for 8-10 minutes or until crisp and lightly browned. Serve with shredded lettuce, salsa and sour cream or other favorite toppings such as enchilada sauce. For children who are finicky eaters, omit the green chilies and onions from the filling.

Carla Lancaster

Mexican Casserole

1   can refried beans with garlic,
    onions and green chilies
1   cup Spanish rice, cooked
4-6 chicken breasts, boneless and
    skinless
water
dash lemon juice

6   tablespoons sour cream
½-¾ jar salsa
cheddar and Monterey Jack cheese,
    shredded
nacho chips, crushed
lettuce, tomatoes, sour cream,
    jalapeño peppers

Combine first two ingredients and spread in casserole. Boil chicken in water with lemon juice until cooked. Remove and cut into bite sized pieces. Sprinkle chicken over bean mixture. Combine sour cream and salsa. Pour over chicken. Sprinkle cheeses over salsa. End with crushed nacho chips. Cover and bake at 375 for 30 minutes. Serve with lettuce, tomatoes, sour cream and jalapeño peppers. Serve with refrigerated corn bread sticks prepared according to package directions.

Marie Dailey, class of 76

Spicy Chicken Quesadillas

4 chicken breasts, skinned and deboned, cut into ¼ inch strips	⅔ cup picante sauce
1 (1¼ ounce) package taco seasoning mix	1 medium sized sweet red pepper, chopped
2½ cups shredded Monterey Jack cheese	10 (10 inch) flour tortillas butter, melted

Combine chicken and taco seasoning mix. Toss to coat. Refrigerate 1 hour. Place chicken in a 15x10x1 inch jelly roll pan. Broil coated chicken 5½ inches from heat, leaving oven door ajar, for 5 minutes. If you prefer, coated chicken may be stir-fried. Cool chicken and cut into bite-sized pieces. Combine chicken, cheese, picante sauce and red pepper, stirring well. Set aside. Brush one side of each tortilla with melted butter. Place two tortillas, buttered side down on a cookie sheet. Top each tortilla with approximately 1 cup chicken mixture, spreading to edges of tortilla. Top each with a tortilla, buttered side up. Bake at 375 for 10 minutes or until golden brown. Cut into wedges. Repeat with remaining tortillas. Serve immediately.

Yield: 5 servings

Janet Buff

Chicken Tortilla Casserole

4-5 chicken breasts, cooked and chopped	1 cup sour cream
1 can cream of mushroom soup	½ teaspoon garlic salt
1 can cream of chicken soup	salt and pepper to taste
1 medium onion chopped fine	¾ (8 ounce) package taco flavored chips, crumbled
2 (3 ounce) cans green chilies, chopped and drained	12 ounces shredded cheddar cheese
	4 tablespoons margarine

Mix all ingredients except cheddar cheese and margarine. Place in a 3 quart casserole dish. Sprinkle with cheese. Dot cheese with margarine. Bake at 350 for 30 minutes.

Yield: 6 servings

Andrea Collier, Tilden Collier, class of 86

Chicken Turnovers

2   cups chicken, cooked and
     chopped
1   (3 ounce) package cream cheese,
     softened
2   tablespoons chopped onion
2   tablespoons snipped chives
2   tablespoons milk
½   teaspoon salt
dash of pepper
1   (8 ounce) package refrigerated
     crescent rolls

Combine chicken, cream cheese, onion, chives, milk, salt and pepper
in medium mixing bowl. Separate rolls into four pieces, sealing
perforations. Pat each piece into a 6 inch square. Spoon ¼ of chicken
mixture onto each square. Bring corners of each square together
over filling and pinch seams together to seal. Using a wide spatula,
transfer turnovers to ungreased baking sheet. Brush with milk. Bake
at 350 for 20-25 minutes or until golden brown.

Yield: 4 servings

Pam Cunningham

Easy No Peas Please
Chicken Pot Pie

1   whole chicken or 4 chicken
     breasts, cooked and cut into bite
     sized pieces
1   can cream of celery soup, fat-free
     works fine
½   cup chicken broth
1½ cups biscuit baking mix
1½ cups milk
1   stick butter or margarine, melted

Place chicken in bottom of 2 quart casserole. Mix soup and broth.
Pour over chicken. Mix biscuit baking mix and milk (will be lumpy
and runny). Pour over chicken soup mixture. Drizzle butter over top.
Bake uncovered at 350 for 1 hour.

Yield: 4-6 servings

Sissy Chesnutt

Easy Chicken Casserole

1   pound chicken breasts, boneless
    and cut into strips
1   can cream of shrimp soup
1   tablespoon sherry

8   ounces Monterey Jack cheese,
    grated
1   cup herb-seasoned stuffing mix
butter

Layer chicken strips in greased casserole dish. Combine soup and sherry and pour over chicken. Sprinkle with cheese. Top with stuffing mix. Dot with butter. Place dish in cold oven. Turn on oven to 350 and bake for 1 hour or until bubbly.

Marty Patterson Chapman, class of 76

Chili-Chicken Casserole

4   ounces tortilla chips, slightly
    crushed
1   pound boneless chicken breasts,
    cut into 1 inch cubes
1   small onion, diced
1   clove garlic, minced
2   tablespoons oil
1   (15 ounce) can tomato sauce
1   (17 ounce) can whole kernel
    corn, drained
1   (15½ ounce) can red kidney
    beans, drained

2   tablespoons chili powder, or to
    taste
¼   teaspoon crushed red pepper
1   teaspoon black pepper
1   tablespoon basil
1   tablespoon parsley
2   cups shredded Monterey
    Jack/cheddar cheese mix
½   cup sliced ripe olives
sour cream

Line bottom of 9x13x2 inch baking dish with chips. In a large skillet, over medium heat, sauté chicken in 1 tablespoon oil until chicken is opaque. Remove from pan and set aside. In same pan, sauté onion and garlic in remaining tablespoon oil until soft, not browned. Stir in chicken and remaining ingredients, except cheeses and olives. Heat until boiling. Pour over chips in pan. Top with cheeses and garnish with olives on top. Bake at 350 for 30 minutes or until heated through and cheeses are melted. Serve with dollop of sour cream.

Yield: 6-8 servings

Linda Peacock

Quick-Topped Vegetable Chicken Casserole

1 (10¾ ounce) can condensed cream of chicken soup	¼ cup chopped green bell pepper
1 (3 ounce) package cream cheese, softened	¼ cup shredded carrot
½ cup milk	1 (9 ounce) package frozen cut broccoli in a pouch, cooked and drained
½ cup chopped celery	2-3 cups cubed cooked chicken
½ cup chopped onion	1 cup buttermilk pancake mix
¼ cup grated Parmesan cheese	

In a medium bowl, combine all ingredients except chicken and pancake mix. Blend well. Place chicken in casserole. Spoon soup mixture over hot chicken. Top with pancake mix. Bake at 375 for 20-30 minutes or until topping is golden brown around edges. This is a good recipe for leftover chicken. It can be made earlier in the day, not baked, refrigerated, then baked as directed for 20-30 minutes for a quick dinner later.

Linda Haven

Fancy Seasoned Turkey Breast

1 (4-6 pound) turkey breast	3 tablespoons garlic salt
butter flavored nonstick cooking spray	1 tablespoon onion powder
3 tablespoons lemon pepper	1 large cooking bag

Skin turkey breast. Rinse and pat dry with paper towels. Spray breast with cooking spray. Combine lemon pepper, garlic salt and onion powder in a bowl. Rub over breast. Place breast side down in bag. Tie clasp very loosely and position hole as close to top of bag as possible to allow steam to escape without putting holes in bag. Microwave 3-4 minutes per pound on high. Turn breast over. Microwave 18-20 minutes more until internal temperature is 170. Let stand 10 minutes before serving.

Anita Watson

Chinese Chicken

1	chicken, cut up	2	tablespoons vinegar
4	tablespoons soy sauce	½	cup brown sugar
¾	cup catsup	1	onion, diced
¾	cup water		

Place chicken in casserole. Mix remaining ingredients and pour over chicken. Bake uncovered at 350 for 1½ hours. Baste occasionally.

Laura Hobbs Lutz, class of 75

Roasted Chicken

6-8	pound chicken	2	carrots, cut in 2 inch pieces
2	tablespoons oil	½	medium onion, chopped
½	tablespoon salt	3	cloves garlic, crushed, optional
1	teaspoon pepper	1	tablespoon butter
2	stalks celery, cut in 2 inch pieces	1	tablespoon flour

Rinse and dry chicken. Tie legs with string. Rub with oil. Sprinkle with salt and pepper. Place chicken in 9x13 pan, breast side up. Scatter vegetables around the chicken. Place pan in 425 preheated oven for 45 minutes. Remove pan and cover with foil, crimping edges to seal. Reduce heat to 325 and continue baking 1½ to 2 hours. Chicken is done when the leg moves easily and juices run clear from the breast. Strain accumulated juices. Press juice from vegetables. Skim off fat. In a bowl, mix 1 tablespoon butter and 1 tablespoon flour. Blend until smooth. Heat juices and whisk in flour and butter mixture. Boil until thickened.

Yield: 6-8 servings

Julie Hoell

Hawaiian Chicken

1   package dry onion soup mix
1   (16 ounce) bottle Russian dressing
1   (12 ounce) jar apricot preserves
1   whole chicken, cut up

Combine soup mix, dressing and preserves. Pour over chicken and bake at 325 for 1 hour.

Yield: 6 servings

Mrs. Loren Edwards

Lemon Dill Chicken

2-3 tablespoons butter or margarine
1   (8 ounce) package fresh mushrooms
1   tablespoon dill weed
2   tablespoons lemon juice
1   teaspoon salt
½   teaspoon paprika
dash of pepper
1   clove garlic, minced
1   whole broiler/fryer, cut up and skinned or 4-6 boneless, skinless chicken breasts
hot cooked rice

Melt butter in large skillet over medium heat. Add mushrooms and cook until done. Add next six ingredients and bring to a boil. Add chicken in a single layer and return to boil. Cover and reduce heat, simmering for 30 minutes or until tender, turning once. Serve over rice.

Yield: 4-6 servings

Lynda Blount

Meats

Winslow
Goins

Breakfast Rolls

1	pound sausage, browned, drained and crumbled	2	packages refrigerated crescent rolls
2	cups shredded cheddar cheese	2	tablespoons butter, melted
2	large eggs, beaten		

In a medium sized bowl, mix together sausage, cheese and eggs. Line a 9x13 inch ovenproof pan with one package crescent rolls. Spread sausage mixture over the crescent dough. Top with the other package of crescent rolls. Crimp the upper and lower edges of dough to seal. Brush the upper crust with butter. Bake at 375 for 20 minutes or until browned.

Yield: 6-8 servings

Betty Lou Trimboli

Holiday Breakfast Casserole

6	large eggs	2	cups shredded cheddar cheese
2	cups milk	6	slices white bread, cubed
1	teaspoon salt	1/3	cup chopped red or green pepper, optional
1	teaspoon dry mustard		
1	(16 ounce) package mild bulk sausage, cooked, drained and crumbled		

In a medium sized bowl, mix together eggs, milk, salt and mustard. Fold in sausage, cheese and bread. Stir in the optional pepper, if desired. Pour mixture into a 9x13 inch casserole. Refrigerate overnight. Remove casserole from refrigerator at least 30 minutes before baking. Bake at 350 for 45 minutes or until set.

Yield: 6 servings

Linda Haven

Susan's Easy Brunch

9	large eggs, beaten	2	cups shredded mild cheddar cheese
3	cups skim milk		
3	slices white bread	2	pounds seasoned bulk breakfast sausage, fried and crumbled
1	teaspoon dry mustard		

In medium bowl, combine eggs and milk. Place bread in bowl with eggs and milk and let sit 5 minutes. Stir to blend. Add remaining ingredients and pour into greased 10x14 inch lasagna pan. Bake at 350 for 1 hour or until set. Easily reheated in microwave in individual servings. Sausage can be cut in half if less is desired.

Yield: 12 servings

Susan King

Spicey Grilled Pork Tenderloin

¼	cup soy sauce	5	garlic cloves, sliced
3	tablespoons brown sugar	2	tablespoons chopped cilantro or parsley
1	teaspoon ground cumin		
1	teaspoon dried mustard	1	pork tenderloin, thin end turned under and tied
½	teaspoon sweet paprika		

Prepare grill or broiler by oiling rack to prevent sticking. Combine first seven ingredients in a zipper plastic bag. Add tenderloin and seal bag. Marinate in refrigerator for 30-60 minutes. Place on grill or under broiler. Baste with marinade and turn halfway through grilling. Tenderloin is done when a meat thermometer reads 160. Let meat repose for 5 minutes to redistribute juices before slicing.

Yield: 3 servings

Carole Cameron

Magic Marinade - Pork

4 cups lemon-lime flavored
   carbonated drink, not diet
1 tablespoon Greek seasoning
salt to taste

1½ teaspoons pepper
3-5 pounds pork chops, tenderloin
   or pork roast

In a large heavy duty resealable plastic bag, mix together drink, Greek seasoning, salt and pepper. Add pork and refrigerate overnight, turning occasionally. Grill or broil pork, basting with marinade, until done.

Yield: 6-8 servings

Daphne Pollock

Basil Pork Chops

4 loin pork chops
1 chicken bouillon cube
½ cup hot water
3 teaspoons vinegar
1 cup fat-free yogurt

salt and pepper to taste
2 tablespoons sugar
1 tablespoon chopped fresh basil
   leaves

Brown pork chops. Dissolve bouillon cube in water. Add remaining ingredients and stir to blend. Place chops in mixture. Bake at 350 for 30 minutes.

Yield: 4 servings

This is great with Red Cinnamon Apples

Joyce Witherington Mattux,
Sea Island Beach Club Spa, class of 77

Born in the Carolina's Chops

1	(16 ounce) cola flavored drink, not diet	1	teaspoon garlic powder
½	cup soy sauce	1	teaspoon ground ginger
1	teaspoon salt	1	teaspoon dried mustard
1	teaspoon ground pepper	6	one inch thick boneless pork chops

In a large, heavy duty, resealable plastic bag, mix first seven ingredients. Shake to blend. Add chops and refrigerate overnight, turning occasionally to coat chops. Grill over low coals until done.

Yield: 4-6 servings

Daphne Pollock

Southern Spareribs

1	cup tomato juice	1	tablespoon Worcestershire sauce
½	cup chopped onion	½	cup vinegar
½	cup brown sugar	¼	cup vegetable oil
1	teaspoon dry mustard	6	pounds pork ribs

Combine all ingredients, except ribs, in a large, heavy duty resealable plastic bag. Shake to blend. Add ribs and refrigerate for 3 hours, turning bag occasionally to coat ribs. Place ribs and marinade in large ovenproof casserole. Cover with foil and bake at 350 for one hour. Remove foil and continue baking, basting every 15 minutes for another hour.

Yield: 6-8 servings

Leraine Collier

Baked Ham with Raisin Sauce

1	3-5 pound picnic ham, cooked	2	teaspoons cornstarch
¾	cup raisins	¼	teaspoon salt
1	cup water	¼	teaspoon ground pepper
4	cloves	1	tablespoon butter
¾	cup brown sugar	1	tablespoon vinegar

In a medium saucepan, combine raisins, water and cloves. Bring to simmer over medium high heat. Simmer for 10 minutes. Mix the sugar, cornstarch, salt and pepper together in a small bowl. Add the mixture to the raisin mixture and stir, heating until thickened. Add butter and vinegar. Remove cloves and serve with prepared ham.

Yield: 6-10 servings

Kathy White

Country Ham

1	whole or half cured ham	water

Rinse and scrub ham. Soak in large pot of warm water for 6 hours. Change the water several times during the soaking period. Place the ham in a roaster, skin side up, with 8-10 cups of water. Cover roaster lightly. Place roaster in a cold oven. Heat the oven to 500. Bake at 500 for 15 minutes. Turn the oven off. Do not open the door. Leave the ham in the oven for 3 hours. Heat the oven again to 500. Bake at 500 for 15 minutes. Turn the oven off. Do not open the door. Leave the ham in the oven for 6-8 hours or overnight. Remove ham from roaster. Skin the ham. Brown the ham under broiler for 5-10 minutes and serve.

This is a super choice for a large group or weekend guests.

Ike and Carol Southerland

Frogmore Stew a la the Gullah House

¼ cup seafood seasoning
4 pounds small red potatoes
2 pounds kielbasa low-fat
  sausage, cut into 1½ inch slices

6 ears fresh corn, halved
4 pounds unpeeled, large fresh
  shrimp
commercial cocktail sauce

Fill large container of a propane cooker halfway with water. Add seafood seasoning. Bring to a boil, following manufacturer's instructions. Add potatoes, sausage and corn. Return to boil and cook 10 minutes or until potatoes are tender. Add shrimp and cook 3-5 minutes or until shrimp turns pink. Remove with slotted spoon onto a serving platter or newspaper lined table. Serve with additional seafood seasoning and cocktail sauce. May also be cooked indoors in a large Dutch oven on a cooktop surface over high heat. A great alternative to a cookout with hot dogs and hamburgers!

Yield: 12 servings

Janet Carson Ricciarelli

Alice's Chili

1 pound ground chuck
2 large onions, chopped
1 green pepper, chopped
2 (15 ounce) cans red kidney
  beans
1 (15 ounce) can tomatoes,
  chopped
1 (8 ounce) can tomato sauce
2½ tablespoons chili powder

2 tablespoons vinegar
1 teaspoon salt
½ teaspoon garlic powder
1 (8 ounce) carton sour cream,
  optional
1½ cups shredded cheddar cheese,
  optional
3 cups cooked rice, optional

In a large pot, over medium high heat, brown ground chuck, onions and pepper. Drain. Add beans, tomatoes, tomato sauce, chili powder, vinegar, salt and garlic powder. Simmer at least 1 hour. As an option, serve over rice and/or top with sour cream and cheese.

Yield: 6 servings

Alice Liles

Cheeseburger Pie

1½ pounds lean ground beef or turkey	2 cups grated cheddar or sharp cheddar cheese
1 medium onion, chopped	2 (9 inch) deep dish pie crusts, thawed
1 (8 ounce) carton sour cream	

In a medium sized skillet, over medium high heat, brown meat and onion. Drain. Let cool briefly. Add sour cream and cheese. Stir to combine. Spoon mixture into one pie crust. Place other crust over mixture, pinching the upper and lower crusts to seal. Cut vents in top of crust. Bake at 400 for 30-40 minutes.

Yield: 4 servings

Amy Hill

Hamburger with Baked Beans

2 slices bacon, diced	½ cup catsup
1 small onion, chopped (optional)	½ teaspoon dry mustard
1 pound lean ground beef	½ teaspoon salt
2 (16 ounce) cans baked beans	dash Worcestershire sauce
¼ cup dark brown sugar	

In large skillet, over medium high heat, cook bacon until crispy. Place bacon in large ovenproof casserole. Place onion in bacon drippings and fry 8-10 minutes. Add onion to casserole with bacon. Brown hamburger in bacon drippings. Drain. Add hamburger to bacon and onions in casserole dish. Add remaining ingredients and stir to mix. Bake at 375 for 30 minutes. Serve with hot rolls.

Yield: 6 servings

Debi Lee

Mexican Casserole

bite size tostida chips
1 pound ground chuck
1 package taco seasoning
1 (16 ounce) carton ricotta cheese
1 jar chunky salsa

1 (8 ounce) carton sour cream
2-3 cups shredded Monterey Jack cheese or 1 package shredded Mexican cheese

Cover bottom of 9x13 inch greased, glass casserole dish with chips. Set aside. Brown ground chuck and add taco seasoning according to directions on package. Spread seasoned meat over chips. Mix ricotta cheese and sour cream and spread over meat. Pour salsa over this. Top with Monterey or Mexican cheese. Bake at 350 for 30 minutes or until cheese is bubbly. Even picky eaters will eat this!

Yield: 4-6 servings

Nancy Deichmann

Mexican Pie

1½ pounds lean ground beef
1 medium onion, chopped
1 (8 ounce) can tomato sauce
1 (10 ounce) can mexicorn
2-3 teaspoons chili powder

salt and pepper to taste
1 (9 inch) deep dish pie crust, baked
1½ cups shredded sharp cheddar cheese

Brown beef and onion. Drain. Add next five ingredients. Simmer 10-15 minutes. Spoon mixture into prepared pie crust. Top with cheese. Bake at 350 for 20 minutes or until the cheese melts. Cool slightly before cutting into wedges to serve.

Yield: 4-6 servings

Martha Flowers

Taco Casserole

2 pounds ground beef	1 (15 ounce) can cream of
3 small onions, diced	mushroom soup
dash garlic powder	12 corn tortillas
1 (4 ounce) can chopped green	1 (10 ounce) can enchilada sauce
chilies, drained	½ pound cheddar cheese, shredded

Brown beef and onions in large skillet. Drain. Stir in garlic powder and green chilies. Pour enchilada sauce into a flat bottom bowl. Dip both sides of 3 tortillas in sauce and place in a greased 9x13 inch casserole dish. Cover with ¼ of the meat mixture, ¼ of the cheese and ¼ of the soup. Repeat layers, beginning with dipped tortillas, until all 12 are used. Pour remaining enchilada sauce over casserole. Top with a sprinkle of cheese and bake at 450 for 20 minutes.

Yield: 8 servings

Penny Pelletier Manning, class of 84

Greek Pizza

1 tablespoon olive oil	1½ teaspoons ground cumin
2 teaspoons minced garlic	1 small can tomato sauce
½ cup finely chopped onion	¼ cup shredded fresh mint
¾ pound lean ground beef	1 refrigerated thick pizza crust
salt and pepper to taste	¾ cup feta cheese

Heat oil, garlic and onion about 2 minutes. Add beef and brown. Drain off fat. Add salt, pepper and cumin. Cook on medium, stirring, for about one minute. Stir in tomato sauce. Cook two more minutes. Add half the shredded mint leaves. Remove from heat and stir gently. Place pizza crust on pan. Top with beef mixture, evenly distributing over crust. Sprinkle with feta cheese. Bake at 450 for 10 minutes. Remove from oven and sprinkle remaining mint on top. Cut and serve. Great with a salad.

Yield: 3-4 normal folks, 2 hungry teens

Vicki Hallberg

Upside Down Pizza

2 pounds hamburger	½ cup sour cream, regular or fat-free
¼ cup chopped onion or 2 tablespoons minced dried onion	1 (8 ounce) can crescent rolls
1 envelope spaghetti sauce seasoning mix	2 tablespoons butter, melted (optional)
1 (16 ounce) can spaghetti sauce	⅓ cup parmesan cheese
1½ cups grated mozzarella cheese or 1 package sliced mozzarella cheese	

Brown beef. Drain. Add onion, sauce mix and sauce. Simmer a few minutes. Spread in a greased 9x13 inch baking dish. Top with sour cream, then mozzarella cheese, then rolls. Brush with butter and sprinkle with parmesan cheese. Bake at 375 for 20 minutes or until brown. A great potluck dish or family supper.

Yield: 5 servings

Cathy Green

Upside Down Pizza

1 (8 ounce) package crescent rolls	1 (1¼ ounce) packet dry spaghetti sauce mix
2 pounds ground beef	1 (8 ounce) carton sour cream
1 cup chopped onions	2 cups shredded mozzarella cheese
2 (8 ounce) cans tomato sauce	

Press crescent rolls into a lightly greased 9x13 inch pan. Brown beef and onion. Drain. Add tomato sauce and dry spaghetti sauce mix. Cover and simmer 10 minutes, stirring frequently. Pour mixture over crescent rolls. Spread sour cream evenly over beef mixture and top with cheese. Bake at 375 for 30-45 minutes or until bubbly. Serve with a tossed salad. This is a real kid pleaser!

Yield: 6-8 servings

Cindy Vainright

Feta Cheese Meatloaf

1   pound ground round
1   packet dried vegetable soup mix

1   (8 ounce) package feta cheese

Mix beef and soup mix. Place ½ mixture in the bottom of a loaf pan. Sprinkle with feta cheese. Top with remaining meat mixture, spreading to sides of pan. Bake at 325 for 25 minutes

Yield: 2-3 servings

Sandra Warren

Pizzaburgers

1   pound hamburger
1   (12 ounce) can spiced luncheon
     meat
1   (15 ounce) container thick
     spaghetti sauce

8   ounces shredded cheddar cheese
dash oregano
hamburger buns
mozzarella cheese

Brown hamburger and luncheon meat. Add remaining ingredients, except buns and mozzarella cheese. Simmer 5 minutes. Spread approximately 3 tablespoons mixture on each hamburger bun half. Sprinkle with mozzarella cheese and place under broiler until cheese melts. May be prepared well in advance and refrigerated or frozen until needed. Spread on buns just before using.

*Donna Knauss,
childhood neighbor of Susan Booth King*

Sweet and Sour Meatloaf

1	(6 ounce) can tomato paste	1	small onion, minced
¼	cup brown sugar	¼	cup crushed crackers
¼	cup vinegar	2	pounds beef
1	teaspoon prepared mustard	1½	teaspoons salt
1	egg, slightly beaten	¼	teaspoon pepper

Mix tomato paste with brown sugar, vinegar and mustard until sugar is dissolved. Combine lightly the egg, onion, crackers, beef, salt, pepper and ½ cup of tomato paste mixture. Shape into loaf. Pour on remaining tomato paste mixture. Bake at 400 for 45 minutes, basting occasionally.

Yield: 4-6 servings

Estelle Jennings

No Mushrooms Salisbury Steak

1	pound ground beef	3	tablespoons olive oil
½	cup quick oatmeal	1	teaspoon beef bouillon granules
2	teaspoons Worcestershire sauce	1	can cream of chicken soup
⅛	teaspoon pepper	1	soup can of water
½	cup vegetable juice		

Combine first five ingredients and shape into four patties. Fry in olive oil until well browned on both sides. Remove from skillet. To drippings in skillet, add remaining ingredients, stirring to blend. Return patties to skillet. Cover and cook 15 minutes, turning once. Serve over rice or egg noodles.

Yield: 4 servings

Susan King

Meatballs

1	pound ground beef	1	package onion soup mix
⅔	cup evaporated milk		oil

Sauce:

1	cup catsup	½	cup brown sugar

Combine beef, milk and soup mix. Shape into small meatballs and brown in hot oil. Drain. Combine catsup and brown sugar. Pour over meatballs. Keep warm in chafing dish or crock pot.

Sharon Hawkins

Beef Stew

2	pounds stewing beef, cubed	1	(18 ounce) can tomato soup, thinned with ½ can water
½	cup sliced carrots		
2	medium onions, chopped	2	medium sized potatoes, cubed
			salt and pepper to taste

Combine all ingredients in casserole dish. Cover tightly and bake at 275 for 5 hours.

Yield: 5-6 servings

Suzanne Moore, class of 82

Baked Round Steak

2	pounds round steak, 1 inch thick	1	(14 ounce) can sliced mushrooms, drained
¼	pound butter, softened	1	envelope dried onion soup mix

Spread butter over steak. Top with mushrooms and soup mix. Wrap steak in double thickness of foil. Place in covered casserole. Bake at 325 for 2 hours.

Yield: 6 servings

Ella Rodgman

Meatball Sandwiches

2	cans prepared spaghetti sauce	2	pounds ground beef
½	cup brown sugar	1	packet meatloaf seasoning
1	teaspoon oregano		packet
1	tablespoon parsley	1	egg

In large pot, heat spaghetti sauce. Add brown sugar, oregano and parsley, stirring to mix. In large bowl, combine beef, seasoning packet and egg. Shape into golf ball sized meatballs. Drop into simmering spaghetti sauce. Gently stir occasionally, cooking 1 hour. Serve with your choice of rolls, bread or over pasta.

Yield: 8 servings

Patricia King McCormick

Baked Beef Stew

3½-4	pounds stew beef, all fat removed	1½	teaspoons sugar
2	cups diced onions	1	can sliced mushrooms (optional)
2	cups celery (large chunks)	2	teaspoons salt or celery salt
2½	cups quartered potatoes	½	teaspoon pepper or lemon pepper
2	cups carrots (large chunks)	4½	tablespoons tapioca
		3	cups vegetable juice

Place all ingredients, in order listed, in roasting pan with tight-fitting lid (no vent). Bake at 250 for 5-6 hours. Do not open oven to stir stew. No browning is necessary. When stew is finished baking, the gravy will be thick and brown.

Yield: 8-10 servings

Estelle Jennings

Grilled Shishkabobs

1 envelope dried onion soup mix	¾ cup water
3 tablespoons sugar	1½ pounds sirloin steak, cut in
¾ cup catsup	1 inch cubes
⅓ cup vinegar	assortment of: cherry tomatoes,
1½ tablespoons mustard	zucchini, squash, green or red
¼ teaspoon salt	peppers, mushrooms, onions
dash hot sauce	

Combine all ingredients, except steak and vegetables. Bring to a boil. Reduce heat and simmer 20 minutes. Cool. Add meat to cooled marinade. Refrigerate overnight. Parboil vegetables if using zucchini squash, peppers, mushrooms or onions. Thread meat and vegetables on skewers, reserving marinade. Grill over medium coals 15-20 minutes. Brush with marinade while grilling. Reheat remaining marinade, bringing to a full boil, if using as dipping sauce.

Use meat tenderizer if desired according to label directions.

Yield: 4-6 servings

Ada Nunn

Pressure Cooker Pot Roast

4 pounds sirloin tip or round	3 cups small new potatoes
roast	2 cups chopped onions
salt, pepper and flour	2 cups water

Sprinkle meat with salt, pepper and flour. Brown meat on both sides in a pressure cooker. Add vegetables and two cups water. Seal the pressure cooker and cook for 20 minutes.

Joyce Witherington Mattux,
Sea Island Beach Club Spa, class of 77

Sensational Sirloin Kabobs

¼ cup soy sauce
3 tablespoons light brown sugar
3 tablespoons vinegar
½ teaspoon garlic powder
½ teaspoon seasoned salt
¼ teaspoon seasoned pepper
⅓ cup lemon-lime soft drink

2 pounds boneless sirloin steak, cut into 1½ inch cubes
½ pound fresh mushroom caps
1 pint cherry tomatoes
2 green peppers, cubed and parboiled
1 small fresh pineapple, cubed

Combine first seven ingredients, mixing well. Pour into a heavy duty plastic zipper bag. Add meat. Marinate overnight in refrigerator, turning bag occasionally. Allow meat to come to room temperature. Thread meat, vegetables and pineapple on skewers, reserving marinade. Grill over medium hot fire 10-15 minutes or until desired degree of doneness, basting frequently with marinade. Serve over a bed of rice, if desired.

Yield: 4 servings

Linda Haven

Flank Steak and Marinade

1 clove crushed garlic
2 teaspoons soy sauce
1 tablespoon vegetable oil
salt and pepper to taste

1 tablespoon catsup
½ teaspoon oregano
flank steak

Mix all ingredients well, except flank steak, and rub on both sides of an average size flank steak. Roll jelly roll style in waxed paper. Refrigerate 24 hours. Charcoal grill is best, or broil 6 minutes on one side, 4 minutes on other side. This marinade is also great with turkey, chicken and pork.

Yield: 6-8 servings

Estelle Jennings

Block Party Beef

6	pound rump roast	¾	cup brown sugar
¼	cup liquid smoke	¼	cup Worcestershire sauce
1	teaspoon garlic powder	2	tablespoons vinegar
1	teaspoon dried minced onion	1½	teaspoons prepared mustard
1	teaspoon salt	1½	teaspoons celery salt
½	teaspoon pepper	1	teaspoon dried minced onion
1	cup water	1	teaspoon salt
1	cup meat juice	½	teaspoon garlic powder
1	(40 ounce) bottle catsup	½	teaspoon pepper

Combine first seven ingredients in a covered roasting pan and bake at 275 for 5-6 hours. Mix and heat remaining ingredients. Tear or chop beef and add sauce. Mix well. Great for a crowd. Serve on hard rolls. Freezes well.

Kathy White

Great Flank Steak

¾	cup vegetable oil	2	tablespoons chopped green onion
¼	cup soy sauce		tops (optional)
¼	cup honey	1	large clove garlic, minced
2	tablespoons vinegar	1½	teaspoons ground ginger
		1½	pound flank steak

Combine all ingredients except steak. Pour into a heavy duty, resealable plastic zipper bag. Add steak and marinate overnight in refrigerator. Grill or broil 5-7 minutes per side. Slice thinly on the diagonal.

Yield: 6 servings

Debi Lee

Korean Beef

1	pound flank steak	1	tablespoon white vinegar
3	tablespoons vegetable oil	2	tablespoons sesame seeds
3	tablespoons soy sauce	¼	cup chopped green onions
2	cloves garlic, minced	1	teaspoon dried ground ginger
1	tablespoon brown sugar		

Combine all ingredients except steak. Mix well. Marinate steak in mixture overnight in refrigerator, turning occasionally. Broil or grill, basting periodically, until desired doneness.

Yield: 4 servings

Ella Rodgman

Easy and Elegant Beef Wellington

4	filet mignons or beef tenderloin cut 1-2 inches thick	1	package of two frozen puff pastry sheets, thawed
1	small can liver pâté		

Brown both sides of filets in skillet over high heat. Turn down heat to low and cook each side four minutes. Remove from pan and cool. Top each filet with liver pâté. Roll pastry sheet on lightly floured surface to thin slightly. Cover each filet with pastry sheet folding edges under. Make decorative top for each filet with leftover pastry using small cookie or biscuit cutters. Place on foil lined baking sheet. Bake at 400 for 20-25 minutes or until golden brown.

Yield: 4 servings

You may brown the filets the day before to save time.

Janet Carson Ricciarelli

Easy Marinade for London Broil

½ cup soy sauce
½ cup vegetable oil
½ cup orange juice
3 teaspoons sugar

½ teaspoon ground ginger
¼ teaspoon garlic salt
¼ teaspoon black pepper

Mix all ingredients in a zippered plastic bag. Shake mixture well to mix. Add 2-4 one to two pound pieces of London Broil roasts. Marinate at least 24 hours. Grill medium rare over medium coals. Slice very thinly with electric knife and serve. Leftovers are great the next day for sandwiches.

Yield: 4-6 servings

Dawn Davis

Marinated London Broil

4-6 pound London broil
1 cup olive oil
2 lemons, juiced
½ cup dry red wine
½ cup dry sherry
2 tablespoons dried oregano

1 tablespoon soy sauce
1 tablespoon honey
1 tablespoon Worcestershire sauce
3 cloves garlic, minced
2 large onions, thinly sliced

Trim most of fat from meat. Pat dry. Combine all other ingredients. Add meat and marinate overnight in refrigerator, turning occasionally. Remove from refrigerator 4 hours before broiling or grilling. Broil or grill to desired doneness. Slice at an angle against the grain.

Yield: 8-10 servings

Crystal Wooten

Beef Tenderloin

1 heaping teaspoon thyme	¼ teaspoon oregano
1 teaspoon black pepper	1 beef tenderloin
1 teaspoon seasoning salt	1 teaspoon table salt
1 teaspoon garlic salt	

Mix spices and rub into meat. Wrap meat in foil and refrigerate overnight or freeze. Take out of refrigerator two hours before cooking. Remove foil and place in pan with water. Sprinkle with table salt and bake at 400 for 25 minutes for rare. Check every five minutes for more well done meat.

Yield: 10 servings

Amy Hill

Barbecue Sauce

32 ounces ketchup	1 tablespoon hot pepper sauce
1¼ cups vinegar	2 tablespoons prepared mustard
1½ cups sugar	2-4 tablespoons Worcestershire sauce
1 cup water	1 tablespoon horseradish
½ bottle garlic salt	

Bring all ingredients to a boil, uncovered. If too thin, add equal amounts of sugar and vinegar. Boil 10-15 minutes.

Elaine Clark Taylor

147

Easy London Broil

1 London broil	cheddar cheese
bottled marinade	croissants

Marinate beef in marinade in a zip lock bag 8 hours or overnight. Grill 5-7 minutes per side for medium rare, depending on the thickness of beef. While beef is grilling, place croissants on cookie sheet in oven at 350 until warm. Remove beef from grill when desired doneness is achieved. Place on cutting board. Top with cheddar cheese, then cover loosely with foil or pot lid until cheese is melted. Using an electric knife, slice beef very thin. Slice croissants. Serve immediately with steak sauce, barbecue sauce, catsup, mayonnaise, or whatever suits you. Quick and so easy!

Yield: 6-10 servings

Susan King

Seafood

Paul Liebstein

Seafood Casserole

1	pound crabmeat	1½	cups finely diced celery
½	cup finely chopped green pepper	1	cup mayonnaise
¼	cup finely chopped onion	½	teaspoon salt
1	tablespoon Worcestershire sauce	2	cups buttered bread cubes
1	pound shrimp, shelled and boiled		

Mix all ingredients except bread cubes and put in a greased casserole. Cover with bread cubes and bake at 350 for 25-30 minutes or until golden.

Ella Rodgman

Crabmeat Soufflé

	nonstick cooking spray	½	cup chopped sweet red pepper (or pimento)
16	slices herb seasoned sandwich bread with crust removed	6	eggs, slightly beaten
4	(6 ounce) packs frozen crabmeat	3½	cups 2% milk
¾	cup mayonnaise	1	can undiluted cream of mushroom soup
1	cup chopped celery		grated Swiss cheese
1	small onion, chopped		paprika
¼	cup chopped green pepper		

Spray 3 quart oblong casserole with nonstick spray. Place 8 slices bread on bottom of casserole. Mix crabmeat, mayonnaise, celery, onion and peppers. Spread evenly on bread. Top with remaining bread. Mix eggs and milk. Pour over all. Place in refrigerator overnight. Bake at 350 for 20 minutes. Remove from oven and spoon soup on top. Bake 40 minutes. Sprinkle Swiss cheese and paprika on top. Reduce heat to 325 and continue baking 25-30 minutes. Allow to cool before cutting.

Yield: 12 servings

Carol Kellum (Marty Vainright's aunt)

AD's Crab Casserole

1	pound fresh crabmeat	2	cup fresh breadcrumbs, finely
2	eggs, beaten		grated
1	cup milk		salt and pepper to taste
¼	stick butter, melted		butter
1	tablespoon Worcestershire sauce		

Mix first five ingredients, 1 cup breadcrumbs, salt and pepper. Place in greased baking dish. Toss remaining 1 cup breadcrumbs with dots of butter and sprinkle over casserole. Bake at 350 for 45 minutes or until lightly browned.

Yield: 4-6 servings

Samia Garner

Shrimp Creole

½	cup chopped onion	1	teaspoon sugar
½	cup chopped celery	1	tablespoon Worcestershire sauce
½	cup chopped green pepper		hot pepper sauce, to taste
1	(16 ounce) can chopped tomatoes	½	teaspoon chili powder (or to taste)
1	(8 ounce) can tomato sauce	1	pound fresh shrimp, peeled and deveined
3	tablespoons oil		
1½	teaspoons salt		

In a large skillet, sauté onion, celery and green pepper in oil. Add tomatoes, tomato sauce, salt, sugar, Worcestershire sauce, hot pepper sauce and chili powder. Simmer, uncovered, for 30 minutes until thickened. Add shrimp. Cover and simmer 5 minutes. Serve over rice.

Yield: 4 servings

Bonnie Everette

Ruth's Crab Cakes

1	pound lump crabmeat	1	tablespoon seafood seasoning
	dash of sea salt	2	large eggs, beaten
	fresh ground black pepper	⅓	cup plain breadcrumbs
1	tablespoon Worcestershire sauce	2	tablespoons butter

With a fork, blend all ingredients, except butter. Form into six 3 inch cakes. In a preheated 5 quart saucepan, add butter. When the butter starts to bubble, add crab cakes. Cook over medium heat until golden brown on both sides.

Yield: 2-4 servings

Samia Garner

Shrimp Kabobs

24-32	large shrimp	2	large bell peppers (green, red or yellow)
1	large can chunk pineapple	1	large onion

Marinade:

¼	cup pineapple juice, drained from chunks	8	ounces tomato sauce
2	tablespoons brown sugar	1	tablespoon mustard
		8	ounces Italian dressing

Peel and clean shrimp, leaving tails on. Drain pineapple, reserving liquid. Cut pepper and onion into chunks. Place all ingredients in a large bowl. Combine marinade ingredients and mix well. Pour over shrimp mixture and marinate at least two hours in refrigerator. Alternate shrimp, pineapple, peppers and onion on skewers. Grill over medium heat. Brush marinade over kabobs while grilling. Serve over rice. You may add scallops also.

Yield: 4-6 servings

Faith Greenwood

Shrimp Destin

¼ cup chopped scallions
2 teaspoons minced garlic
1 cup butter or margarine
2 pounds large shrimp, peeled and deveined
1 teaspoon lemon juice
1 tablespoon white wine
½ teaspoon salt
coarsely ground black pepper
1 teaspoon dried whole dill weed
1 teaspoon chopped fresh parsley
3 French rolls, split lengthwise and toasted

Sauté scallions and garlic in butter until scallions are tender. Add shrimp, lemon juice, wine, salt and pepper. Cook over medium heat about 5 minutes, stirring occasionally. Stir in dill weed and parsley. Spoon mixture over toasted rolls and serve immediately.

Yield: 6 servings

Janet Carson Ricciarelli

Shrimp with Pears and Pernod

2 tablespoons butter
2 scallions, minced (white parts only)
½ pound shrimp, peeled and deveined
1 small pear, cored and cut into thin wedges
1 teaspoon cracked black pepper
¼ teaspoon salt
¼ cup Pernod (Anise flavored liqueur)
2 tablespoons heavy cream

In a heavy skillet, melt butter. Add scallions and shrimp. Cook 2 minutes over medium heat, stirring occasionally. Add pear, pepper and salt. Toss gently. Pour in Pernod and ignite. Shake pan until flame dies out. Add cream and stir gently for 1 minute.

Yield: 2 servings

Samia Garner

Shrimp and Cheese Casserole

6	slices white bread without crust	¼	cup butter, melted
½	pound extra sharp cheddar cheese	½	teaspoon dry mustard
			salt to taste
1	pound cooked and cleaned shrimp	3	eggs, beaten
		1	pint milk

Break bread and cheese into bite size pieces. Arrange shrimp, bread and cheese in several layers in a greased casserole dish. Pour melted butter over. Mix eggs, mustard, salt and milk. Pour over other ingredients. Cover and let stand overnight in refrigerator. Bake at 350 for 1 hour or until firm.

Yield: 6 servings

Marty Vainright

Emmett's Fish Stew

2	pounds slab bacon	1	can tomato paste
10	pounds potatoes	2	cans tomato sauce
5	pounds onions	2	dozen eggs (or at least one per person)
5	pounds rock fish filet		
crushed red pepper, salt and pepper to taste			

Cut slab bacon into 1 inch pieces. Fry in skillet. Set aside. Slice potatoes and onions ½ inch thick. In large pot pour in bacon and dripping. Layer potatoes, onions and fish. Continue with layers until all are used, ending with fish. Add crushed red pepper, salt and pepper. Mix tomato paste and tomato sauce. Pour over layers. Add enough water to cover ingredients in pot. Bring to a boil over medium heat. Cook until potatoes are tender. Do not stir. Break eggs and put in one at a time. Let set for 15 minutes after eggs are done. Repeat, do not stir. Use a large spoon or dipper, going straight to the bottom of pot and coming up. This way you will get some of each ingredient and will not make the stew mushy. It is customary to prepare stews in black iron wash pots over an outdoor fire.

Yield: 10-15 servings

Chad Reynolds (grandfather's recipe)

Class of 90

Sailing Stew

2	pounds small to medium shrimp	3	(6½ ounce) cans minced clams
1	pound crabmeat		or 2 (8 ounce) cans whole clams
	margarine to sauté	¾	cup vermouth to taste
2	(19 ounce) cans chunky New	2	(10½ ounce) cans she-crab soup
	England clam chowder or	2	cups milk
	chunky vegetable soup		garlic, salt and pepper to taste
		½	cup finely chopped fresh parsley

Sauté shrimp and crabmeat in butter. Add remaining ingredients and simmer 15-20 minutes. Do not allow to boil. Serve immediately. You may add any of your favorite seafoods to this recipe. This recipe may be doubled. Good reheated.

Yield: 6 servings

Sarah Exum Edwards

Citrus Grilled Salmon

4	salmon steaks, 1 inch thick	1	tablespoon honey
¼	cup soy sauce	2	cloves garlic, minced
1	teaspoon grated lime rind	2	tablespoons minced fresh chives
2	tablespoons lime juice		

Place salmon in large shallow dish. Combine next four ingredients. Pour over salmon, turning to coat. Cover and refrigerate 30 minutes, turning once. Remove fish from marinade, reserving liquid. Grill fish over medium-hot coals (350-400) 3 minutes on each side or until fish flakes easily when tested with fork, basting frequently with reserved marinade. Transfer to serving platter and sprinkle with chives.

Yield: 4 servings

Janet Carson Ricciarelli

Sonora Salmon

2	pounds salmon filets or 3-4 steaks	2	dashes pepper
1	teaspoon fresh dill, dry may be used	2	tablespoons sliced mushrooms, optional
2	tablespoons grated onion	¾	cup light cream

Clean fish and pat dry. Place in a single layer in a greased baking dish. Mix remaining ingredients, except cream, and sprinkle over fish. Pour cream over fish. Bake at 375 for 20 minutes. Test after 12-15 minutes with a fork if steaks are 1 inch thick. Fish should flake easily when tested.

Yield: 4 servings

Samia Garner

Easy Salmon Loaf

1½	cups skim milk	1	(16 ounce) can salmon
1	slice bread	½	teaspoon salt
4	tablespoons butter	1	tablespoon dried onion flakes
2	eggs, beaten		

Heat milk, bread and butter in medium saucepan until creamy. Remove from heat and add remaining ingredients. Pour into greased loaf pan. Bake at 350 for 1 hour or until firmly set. Cool in pan five minutes before serving. Reheats easily in microwave.

Yield: 6 servings

Joyce Gaudet Booth, mother of Susan King

156

Margarita Grilled Salmon

4	pounds salmon steaks, ½ inch thick		1	teaspoon salt
3	tablespoons minced garlic		4	limes, reserve 1 for garnish

Mix garlic and salt. Spread on fish. Squeeze lime juice over fish. Marinate two hours. Oil grill. Grill 7-10 minutes on each side, depending on thickness. Serve with vegetable kabobs and potato steaks.

Joyce Witherington Mattux,
Sea Island Beach Club Spa, class of 77

Grilled Tuna with Cilantro Butter

6	tuna steaks, ¾ inch thick		2	tablespoons minced green onion
½	cup brown sugar		2	tablespoons minced gingerroot
½	cup soy sauce		2	teaspoons garlic
½	cup water		¼	teaspoon crushed red pepper
¼	cup vegetable oil			

Cilantro Butter:

¼	cup plus 2 tablespoons butter, softened		1	teaspoon minced garlic
¼	cup fresh cilantro leaves, loosely packed		2	teaspoons gingerroot

In food processor, combine butter, cilantro leaves, gingerroot and garlic. Process until smooth. Shape into log and wrap in wax paper. Chill until firm. Place tuna steaks in shallow dish. Combine remaining ingredients and mix well to make marinade. Pour over steaks. Marinate at least one hour or longer. Reserve marinade. Place steaks on grill over medium to hot coals. Grill covered 4-6 minutes each side or until fish flakes. Baste occasionally with marinade. Slice chilled butter into 6 pieces and place on each tuna steak when served. Garnish with cilantro sprigs.

Yield: 6 servings

Faith Greenwood

Tempting Italian Tuna Melts

1	(6 ounce) can tuna in water, drained	½	teaspoon dried oregano
⅓	cup nonfat mayonnaise	2	English muffins, split and toasted
¼	cup chopped onion	4	tomato slices
¼	cup chopped green pepper	4	slices mozzarella or Swiss cheese
½	teaspoon dried basil		

Mix tuna, mayonnaise, onion, green pepper and spices. Spoon tuna mixture over English muffins. Top each with tomato slice. Place on cookie sheet. Broil 1 minute. Top each with cheese slice. Sprinkle with parsley. Broil 1-2 minutes or until cheese begins to melt.

Yield: 4 servings

Debbie Gaskins

Tuna Chopstick

1	can mushroom soup	½	cup cashews
¼	can water	¼	cup chopped onion
13	ounce can chow mein noodles		dash pepper
1	cup canned tuna	1	can mandarin oranges, optional
1	cup diced celery		

Combine soup and water. Add one cup of noodles, tuna, celery, cashews, onion and pepper. Place in ungreased baking dish. Add remaining noodles on top. Bake at 375 for 15-20 minutes or until hot. Garnish with canned mandarin oranges if desired.

Ella Rodgman

Vegetables & Fruits

J Johnson

Baked Beans

1	(16 ounce) can pork and beans, drained	1	teaspoon chili powder
1	small onion, chopped	4	tablespoons molasses
1	green pepper, chopped		catsup, to taste
1	teaspoon mustard	2	slices bacon (optional)

Combine all ingredients except bacon. Place in a greased 2 quart casserole. Lay bacon on top. Bake uncovered at 350 for 30-40 minutes or until mixture thickens and bacon is cooked. Great for pot luck dinners and picnics.

Yield: 4-6 servings

Alice Liles

Swiss Beans

2	tablespoons butter	1	cup sour cream
2	tablespoons flour	2	cans French-style green beans, drained or 4 cups fresh beans
½	teaspoon salt		
¼	teaspoon pepper	½	pound Swiss cheese, grated
1	teaspoon sugar	1	cup cracker crumbs
½	teaspoon grated onion	4	tablespoons butter, melted

Melt butter, stir in flour, salt, pepper, sugar and onions. Add sour cream gradually. Fold in green beans. Pour into greased casserole. Sprinkle cheese over beans. Combine cracker crumbs with butter and sprinkle over cheese. Bake at 400 for 20 minutes.

Betty Lou Trimboli

Broccoli Casserole

2   packages frozen broccoli, cooked
1   can cream of mushroom soup
1   cup mayonnaise
1   egg
1   small onion, finely chopped

salt and pepper to taste
cheddar cheese, shredded
small package stuffing mix
¼   cup butter, melted

Mix together all ingredients, except stuffing mix and melted butter. Pour into casserole dish. Mix stuffing mix and melted butter and place on top of broccoli mixture. Bake at 350 for 30 minutes.

Joan Braswell

Broccoli Casserole

2   (10 ounce) packages broccoli
    florets, cooked
1   stick butter, melted
1   cup instant rice

1   jar pasteurized processed cheese
    spread
1   can cream of mushroom soup

Place broccoli in 9x13 inch baking dish. Combine butter, rice, cheese spread and soup. Bake at 350 for 30 minutes.

Yield: 10-12 servings

Carole Cameron

Quick Broccoli with Cheese

2   bunches broccoli, washed and
    cut into small pieces

1   (10¾ ounce) can cream of
    mushroom soup
½-1 cup shredded cheddar cheese

Cook broccoli in ½ cup water in covered container in microwave on high for 10 minutes, or until tender. Drain. Spoon soup over broccoli and top with cheese. Microwave on high 1-2 minutes or until cheese melts.

Yield: 6 servings

Janet Carson Ricciarelli

Baked Creamed Cabbage

1	medium sized head cabbage	½	teaspoon salt
½	cup water, salted and boiling	1½	cups milk
3	tablespoons butter or margarine	¼	cup bread crumbs
3	tablespoons flour		

Shred cabbage finely and cook 9 minutes in salted water. Drain and place in a buttered 1½ quart casserole. Melt butter in saucepan. Stir in flour and salt until smooth. Add milk gradually. Continue stirring until mixture thickens. Pour sauce over cabbage and sprinkle bread crumbs over top. Bake at 325 about 15 minutes or until crumbs are browned.

Ella Rodgman

Summer Cantaloupe

1	cantaloupe per person	1	jigger whiskey per cantaloupe
	canned fruit cocktail		

Cut 3 inch plug in top of cantaloupe and remove, reserving plug. Remove seeds. Add fruit cocktail and whiskey. Replace plug and refrigerate overnight. Serve with a spoon.

Warren and Judy Johnson

Corn Pudding

¾	stick butter	½	cup sugar
2	tablespoons flour	1	cup milk
2	eggs, slightly beaten		nutmeg, to taste
1	can creamed corn		

Melt butter. Whisk flour into butter and add remaining ingredients. Beat well with spoon. Bake in 375 oven until it shakes a little in center. (1 hour or more)

Elaine Clark Taylor

Zesty Carrots

6-8 carrots, cut into lengthwise strips and cooked
¼ cup carrot water
2 tablespoons horseradish
½ cup mayonnaise
½ teaspoon salt
¼ teaspoon pepper
⅓ cup bread crumbs moistened with melted butter (I use crushed no fat croutons instead)

Place carrots in shallow casserole dish. Combine remaining ingredients and pour over carrots. Top with bread crumbs. Bake at 325 for 15-20 minutes.

Yield: 4-6 servings

Evelyn Deane

Corn Pudding

3 eggs
⅔ cup sugar
dash salt
2 tablespoons flour
2 cups frozen or canned corn
1 cup canned evaporated milk
4 tablespoons butter, melted
2 ounces chopped pimento

Beat eggs, sugar, salt and flour together. Add corn, milk, butter and pimento. Pour into buttered casserole. Bake at 350 for 35 minutes or until lightly browned.

Yield: 6-8 servings

Martha Flowers

Corn Pudding

¼ cup flour
⅓ cup sugar
3 eggs, beaten
(15 ounce) can cream style corn
1 cup milk
2 tablespoons butter, melted

Mix flour, sugar and eggs. Stir in corn, milk and butter. Pour into greased casserole dish. Bake uncovered at 350 for 1 hour.

Yield: 4-5 servings

Dinah Sylivant

Cranberry-Apple Bake

3	cups red apples, unpeeled and sliced	½	cup pecans, chopped
2	cups raw cranberries	⅓	cup flour
1	cup sugar	½	cup brown sugar
1	cup quick oats, uncooked	1	stick margarine, melted

Combine apples and cranberries in 2 quart casserole dish. Mix remaining ingredients, except margarine, and spread over apples and cranberries. Spoon melted margarine over top. Bake at 325 for 45-60 minutes. Can be used with a meal or as a dessert with whipped topping. Freezes well.

Yield: 6-8 servings

Jean Jones

Curried Fruit

1	large can pear halves	1	cup maraschino cherries
1	large can peach halves	¼	cup butter, melted
1	medium can pineapple chunks	1	cup brown sugar
2	small cans mandarin orange sections	4	teaspoons curry powder

Drain fruit, mix together and place in casserole dish. Combine butter, brown sugar and curry powder. Dribble butter mixture over fruit. Bake at 350 for 45-60 minutes. Great accompaniment for poultry entrées.

Nancy Bowers

Fresh Fruit Sauce

1	(8 ounce) package cream cheese, softened	⅛	teaspoon salt
2	tablespoons mayonnaise	¼	cup orange juice
3	tablespoons sugar	¼	cup pineapple juice

In food processor or electric mixer, blend cream cheese, mayonnaise, sugar and salt. Add juices and mix well. Chill at least one hour. Serve over fresh fruit.

Nancy Bowers

Mushroom Casserole

1½ pounds sliced mushrooms
1 medium onion, chopped
½ cup butter
2 tablespoons flour
1 cup sour cream (low fat or fat-free may be used)

salt and pepper to taste
2 tablespoons chopped fresh parsley
¼ cup bread crumbs
¼ cup butter

Sauté mushrooms and onion in butter until onion is transparent. Stir in flour and cook 5-10 minutes over low heat. Blend in sour cream, salt and pepper. Stir in chopped parsley. Place in shallow 1½ quart buttered casserole. Sprinkle with bread crumbs and dot with remaining butter. Bake uncovered at 350 for 25 minutes.

Yield: 6-8 servings

Martha Flowers

Almond-Onion Casserole

2 (15½ ounce) jars whole onions
1½ tablespoons butter or margarine
1½ tablespoons flour
½ cup mushroom soup (½ can)

½ cup shredded sharp cheddar cheese
¼ cup toasted almonds
¼ cup sherry

Drain onions and place in buttered 1 quart casserole. In small pan, melt butter and stir in flour, soup, cheese, almonds and sherry. Stir until smooth and pour over onions. (Optional: sprinkle with additional almonds) Bake uncovered at 350 for 30 minutes or until bubbly.

Yield: 6 servings

Cathy Green

Baked Onions

12 medium sized fresh onions, sliced
1 (3¾ ounce) bag potato chips, crushed
½ pound Wisconsin mild cheese, grated
2 cans cream of mushroom soup
½ cup milk
⅛ teaspoon cayenne pepper

In a 9x13 inch buttered casserole, place alternate layers of thinly sliced onions, potato chips and grated cheese. Mix soup and milk. Pour over onion mixture. Sprinkle with pepper. Bake 1 hour at 350. Good with barbecue.

Yield: 12-15 servings

Kay Gross

Cheesy Vidalia Onion Casserole

½ cup butter or margarine, melted
5-6 Vidalia onions, sliced
Parmesan cheese
¾ cup round cracker crumbs, divided
¾ cup cheese cracker crumbs, divided
salt and pepper to taste
1 (10¾ ounce) can cream of mushroom soup, undiluted
1 cup grated cheddar cheese
paprika

Sauté onions in butter. In a 1½ quart casserole, layer half of onions. Top with Parmesan, half of cracker crumbs, half of cheese cracker crumbs, salt and pepper. Repeat layers in order beginning with remaining onions. Spread soup on top. Sprinkle with cheddar cheese and Parmesan cheese. Garnish with paprika. Bake at 350 for 30 minutes.

Yield: 8-10 servings

Evelyn Deane

Bleu Cheese Crusted Onions

2	pounds Spanish onions	3	teaspoons Worcestershire sauce
8	ounces bleu cheese, crumbled	1	teaspoon dried dill weed
6	tablespoons margarine at room temperature		freshly ground black pepper

Slice onions and place in buttered baking dish. Combine remaining ingredients, using scraper to clean sides of bowl. Spread over onions using large spatula. Bake in center of oven at 425 for 20 minutes. Broil briefly until top is brown and bubbly. Great with barbecued meat.

Yield: 6-8 servings

Evelyn Deane

Golden Baked Onion Casserole

6	medium onions, thinly sliced		salt and pepper to taste
1	stick margarine	12	ounces Swiss cheese, shredded
1	can cream of chicken soup		French bread
1	cup milk		

Sauté onions in 2 tablespoons margarine until tender. Remove with slotted spoon and put into 9x13 inch casserole dish. Set aside. Mix together soup, milk, salt and pepper. Pour over onions. Top with cheese. Slice the bread. Melt remaining margarine. Dip one side of each slice of bread in margarine. Place each slice, buttered side up, over the onion-cheese mixture. Bake at 350 for 30-40 minutes or until bubbly and bread is golden.

Mrs. Loren Edwards

Baked Vidalia Onions

4   Vidalia onions
¼   cup water
2-3 tablespoons balsamic vinegar

salt and pepper to taste
several pats butter

Peel and trim onions. Slice ¼ inch from the top. Place in baking dish, cut side up. Add water and vinegar. Season with salt and pepper. Dot with butter. Bake at 350 for 1 hour or until tender. Baste with juices while baking. Add more water if necessary.

Yield: 4 servings

Betty Lou Trimboli

Paul's Marinated Vidalias

2   medium Vidalia onions
1   cup water
½   cup sugar
¼   cup white vinegar

1   tablespoon plus 1 teaspoon
     mayonnaise
1   teaspoon celery seeds
lettuce leaves

Slice onions and separate into rings. Combine water, sugar and vinegar. Stir until sugar dissolves. Pour over onion rings. Cover and chill at least 3 hours. Drain. Stir in mayonnaise and celery seeds. Serve on lettuce leaves.

Yield: 4 servings

Betty Lou Trimboli

Roasted Onions

2-3 large Vidalia onions
3   tablespoons extra-virgin olive oil
2   tablespoons garlic, chopped
1   teaspoon salt, or to taste

½   teaspoon freshly ground black
     pepper
½   cup fresh mint
¼   cup balsamic vinegar

Remove onion skins and trim ends. Cut in half from stem to root end. Mix olive oil, garlic, salt, pepper and mint. Coat onions with mixture and place in roaster. Bake at 350 for 30 minutes. Baste with juices and continue roasting another 15 minutes or until soft. Drizzle generously with vinegar.

Yield: 4 servings

Betty Lou Trimboli

French Onion Casserole

4	medium onions, sliced	1½	cups plain croutons tossed with
3	tablespoons butter or margarine		two tablespoons melted butter
2	tablespoons flour	2	ounces Swiss or Monterey Jack
¾	cup beef bouillon		cheese, grated
¼	cup dry sherry	3	tablespoons grated Parmesan
			cheese

Cook onions in butter until tender. Blend in flour and pepper. Add sherry and bouillon and cook until bubbly. Turn into 1 quart casserole. Cover with croutons and cheese. Heat in oven until cheese melts.

Yield: 4-6 servings

Kay Gross

Pea Casserole Supreme

3	tablespoons margarine	1	(10¾ ounce) can cream of
2	small scallions, finely chopped		mushroom soup
1½	cups finely chopped celery	2	tablespoons milk
2	packages frozen peas or 1 family size	¾	cup soft bread crumbs or herbseasoned stuffing
1	can water chestnuts, drained and sliced		cooking spray

Sauté scallions and celery in butter in microwave until tender, 1-3 minutes on high. Add all other ingredients except bread crumbs. Mix well. Spoon into casserole dish, sprayed with cooking spray. Sprinkle with bread crumbs or stuffing. Bake, uncovered, at 350 for 30 minutes.

Yield: 6-8 servings

Janet Carson Ricciarelli

Low Fat Unfried Fries

4-5	large baking potatoes	2	large egg whites
	cooking spray	1	tablespoon Cajun spice

Slice potatoes lengthwise into French fries. Coat baking sheet with three sprays of cooking spray. Combine egg whites and Cajun spice in a bowl. Add potatoes a few at a time to coat well. Spread on baking sheet, leaving a little space between. Shake more Cajun spice over to dust well. Bake at 400 for 40 minutes, until crispy, turning every 10 minutes with a spatula so they brown evenly.

Yield: 4 servings

Ada Nunn

Cheesy Creamed Potatoes

8	medium white potatoes	4	ounces sour cream
3	tablespoons finely chopped onions	½	stick butter, melted
		1	cup shredded cheddar cheese
3	ounces cream cheese	½	cup bacon bits

Boil peeled and sliced potatoes in salted water until done. Combine onions, cream cheese, sour cream and butter in large mixing bowl. Pour the cooked potatoes into strainer and then add them to other ingredients while HOT. Use mixer to combine all ingredients until smooth and creamy. Pour into greased casserole or baking dish. Cover with cheddar cheese and bacon bits. Bake at 350 for 30 minutes.

Yield: 6-8 servings

Kay Allen Blizzard, class of 74

Crusty Baked Potatoes

4	baking potatoes	1	teaspoon salt
4	tablespoons butter	1	teaspoon paprika
1	cup fine bread crumbs		

Wash and peel potatoes, leaving them whole. Pat dry. Melt butter in saucepan. Roll potatoes in butter then coat evenly with bread crumbs which have been mixed with salt and paprika. Place potatoes in shallow greased casserole. Cover and bake at 400 for one hour or until tender. (Any butter left from coating the potatoes may be added to the bottom of the casserole.) For the last 20 minutes, remove cover and turn potatoes to brown evenly.

Yield: 4 servings

Linda Page

Hashbrown Potato Casserole

cooking spray		1	(32 ounce) package frozen hash
1	can cream of mushroom soup		brown potatoes
1	(16 ounce) container sour	½	cup chopped onion
	cream	2	cups shredded cheese, divided
1	teaspoon salt	1	stick margarine, melted
¼	teaspoon pepper	cornflakes	

Mix together soup, sour cream, salt and pepper. Add potatoes, onions, 1 cup cheese and margarine. Mix well. Pour into casserole pan, sprayed with cooking spray. Bake at 350 for 1 hour. Remove from oven. Sprinkle with remaining 1 cup cheese, then cover with cornflakes.

Yield: 6-8 servings

Paige Smith Hutto, class of 89

Hash Brown Casserole

2 pounds frozen hash browns	1 pound shredded cheese
½ onion, chopped	16 ounces sour cream
2 cans cream of chicken soup	

Topping:

1 stick margarine, melted	2 cups crushed round crackers

Mix all ingredients together and place in a 9x13 inch dish. Top with cracker and margarine mixture. Bake at 350 for 1 hour and 15 minutes.

Yield: 6-8 servings

Beth Sanderson

Cheesy New Potatoes

12 medium new potatoes	8 slices bacon, cooked and crumbled
1 cup grated sharp cheese	(can substitute bacon bits)
(amount can be varied to taste)	½ cup margarine, melted
	salt and pepper to taste

Wash potatoes, but do not peel. Slice into ¼ inch slices. Cook in boiling water until done, but not mushy. Drain and set aside. Spray 2 quart casserole dish with nonstick cooking spray. Layer ingredients using ½ potatoes, ½ cheese, ½ bacon and ½ butter. Sprinkle with salt and pepper. Layer remaining ingredients in the same fashion. Heat in 400 oven for 15-20 minutes.

Yield: 8 servings

Carol Southerland

Potato Steaks

3 potatoes	2 cans beef broth

Cut potatoes in strips. Place in baking dish. Pour broth over potatoes. Bake at 400 until broth has soaked into potatoes.

Joyce Witherington Mattux,
Sea Island Beach Club Spa, class of 77

Hashbrown Cheese Bake

1   (32 ounce) package hash
    browns, thawed
2   (10¾ ounce) cans cream of
    potato soup

2   (8 ounce) containers fat free
    sour cream
1   cup shredded cheddar cheese
1   cup grated Parmesan cheese
1   cup shredded mozzarella cheese

Combine all ingredients, stirring well. Spoon into a 9x13 inch greased baking pan. Bake at 350 for 40 minutes or until lightly browned.

Yield: 10-12 servings

Janet Carson Ricciarelli

New Potatoes with Lemon and Chives

2   pounds new potatoes, unpeeled
¼   cup butter or margarine
2   tablespoons chopped chives

salt to taste
grated peel of 1 lemon
2   tablespoons lemon juice

Cook cleaned potatoes in salted water. Drain and quarter. Add remaining ingredients. Heat thoroughly.

Betty Lou Trimboli

Potato Pancakes

6-7 potatoes, grated
1   egg
1   large onion, grated
salt and pepper to taste

½   teaspoon baking powder
all-purpose flour
cooking oil

Mix first five ingredients in large bowl. Gradually add flour until mixture has a creamy consistency. Heat oil in heavy skillet or electric frying pan at 350. Drop heaping tablespoons of mixture into pan, flatten and fry until golden brown. Serve with soup and salad.

Yield: approximately 20 pancakes

Hudock Family

Ranch Potatoes

5-6 large potatoes, cut into bite-sized 2 teaspoons dill weed
    cubes salt and pepper to taste
⅓ cup prepared ranch dressing

Boil potatoes, seasoned with salt and pepper, for approximately 12-13 minutes until tender. Drain. Stir in dressing and dill weed. Serve hot as a side dish or refrigerate and serve as cold potato salad. Serve as a complement to roast beef, steak, lamb chops, barbecued chicken or buffalo wings.

Yield: 4 servings

Jo Allen, class of 76

Scalloped Potatoes

¼ cup chopped onion 1¼ cup milk
2 tablespoons butter ¾ cup sharp cheddar cheese
2 tablespoons flour 3 medium potatoes, peeled and
½ teaspoon salt   thinly sliced
½ teaspoon pepper

Sauté onion in butter until tender. Add flour, salt, pepper and milk. Cook and stir until sauce thickens and is bubbly. Add cheese and stir until melted. Remove from heat. In a greased 1 quart casserole dish, place half of the potatoes. Cover with half the sauce, then remaining potatoes and sauce. Bake covered at 350 for 35 minutes or until potatoes are tender. Sprinkle additional cheese on top if desired. Let cool 5 minutes before serving.

Yield: 4 servings

Sallie Edwards Mayeux, class of 88

Sour Cream Potatoes

8-10 medium potatoes
1   cup sour cream
1   (8 ounce) package cream cheese
2   tablespoons chopped chives

salt and pepper to taste
butter
paprika

Cook potatoes until tender. Mash potatoes in mixer. Add sour cream, cream cheese, chives, salt and pepper. Spread in casserole. Dot with butter and paprika. Bake at 350 for 20 minutes or until heated thoroughly.

Yield: 8-10 servings

Leraine Collier

Senator Russell's Sweet Potatoes

3   cups boiled sweet potatoes, mashed (canned are fine)
2   eggs
3/4 cup sugar
1   stick margarine, melted

1   teaspoon vanilla
1   cup chopped pecans
1/2 cup brown sugar
1/3 cup flour
1/3 cup margarine, NOT melted

Combine first five ingredients and put in a 9x9 inch baking dish. Mix remaining ingredients and pour over potatoes. Bake at 350 until firm, about 30 minutes.

Kathy Sawyer

Spinach Casserole

1   can artichoke hearts
2   packages frozen spinach, cooked 2 minutes and drained
2   small packages cream cheese, softened

6   ounces butter
dash of salt
2   tablespoons lemon juice
bread crumbs

Line greased casserole with artichoke hearts. Mix all remaining ingredients except bread crumbs. Pour over artichoke hearts. Top with bread crumbs. Bake at 350 about 30 minutes.

Ella Rodgman

Sweet Potato Casserole

3	cups cooked sweet potatoes, cooled	⅓	cup skim milk or evaporated skim milk
⅓	cup sugar	½	cup orange juice
4	egg whites, beaten (can use egg substitute)	¼	cup margarine
1	tablespoon vanilla	½	cup pecans
		¾	cup brown sugar
		½	cup flour

Mix first six ingredients and spread in a greased 9x13 inch baking pan. In small bowl, combine remaining ingredients, mixing well. Sprinkle over casserole. Bake at 350 for 30 minutes. Serve with ham, chicken or turkey.

Dinah Sylivant

Tomato Pie

1	(9 inch) pie shell, baked	2	cups grated sharp cheddar cheese
3-5	peeled, sliced and drained tomatoes	¼	cup chopped onion
	salt and pepper to taste	½	teaspoon basil
½	cup mayonnaise	8	round butter crackers, crumbled
		2	teaspoons butter, melted

Arrange tomato slices in bottom of baked pie shell. Sprinkle with salt and pepper. Mix mayonnaise, cheese, onion and basil. Spread on tomatoes. Combine cracker crumbs and melted butter. Sprinkle over tomatoes. Bake at 400 for 35 minutes. Serve immediately.

Sissy Chesnutt

Layered Spinach Supreme

1	cup biscuit baking mix	½	cup grated Parmesan cheese
¼	cup milk	4	ounces Monterey Jack cheese
2	eggs	12	ounces cottage cheese
½	cup chopped onion		salt to taste
1	package frozen spinach, thawed	1	teaspoon garlic

Combine biscuit baking mix with milk, eggs and onion. Spread in a 9x13 inch baking dish. Combine remaining ingredients and pour over biscuit mixture. Bake at 375 for 30 minutes.

Lisa Mumford Kluttz, class of 88

Tomato Pie

⅓	cup chopped onion	8	ounces grated white cheese, or
⅓	cup mayonnaise		½ yellow and ½ mozzarella
½	teaspoon oregano	2	deep dish pie crusts
½	teaspoon basil	2	(28 ounce) cans plum tomatoes,
½	teaspoon salt		drained
	freshly ground pepper		

In a food processor, using the steel blade, mix onion, mayonnaise, herbs, salt and pepper. Blend in cheese. In a quiche pan or large flat oven proof bowl, place your first crust, overlapping edge of bowl. Spread in half of cheese mixture. Add drained tomatoes. Top with remaining cheese mixture, spreading evenly. Top with remaining crust. Crimp edge and cut a steam vent in center. Bake at 400 for 30 minutes or until browned and bubbly. Best if baked early in the day and reheated in a 350 oven. Also, if using fresh herbs, double the amount listed.

Julie Hoell

Tomato Pie

1	9 inch deep dish pie shell		garlic powder to taste
5	large tomatoes, peeled and thickly sliced	¾	cup mayonnaise
½	teaspoon salt	1¼	cups grated mozzarella or Swiss cheese
½	teaspoon pepper		thinly sliced onions (optional)
3	teaspoons dried basil		

Bake pie shell 10 minutes at 375. Layer tomatoes in shell, sprinkling each layer with salt, pepper, basil and garlic powder. Combine mayonnaise and cheese. Spread over tomatoes (and onions, if used). Bake at 350 for 35 minutes or until brown. Allow to stand at least 5 minutes before serving.

Betty Lou Trimboli

Roasted Veggies

10	tiny new potatoes, quartered	1	red pepper, sliced
1	cup peeled and sliced carrots	1	green pepper, sliced
1	onion, cut into wedges		

Marinade:

¼	cup olive oil	1	teaspoon dried rosemary
3	tablespoons lemon juice		salt and pepper to taste
3	cloves garlic, minced		

In large zip-top plastic bag, combine all marinade ingredients and mix well. Add vegetables and marinate several hours or overnight. Place potatoes, carrots and onions in a 9x13 inch glass casserole dish. Bake at 450 for 35 minutes. Add peppers and cook an additional 15-20 minutes.

Yield: 4 servings

Sallie Edwards Mayeux, class of 88

178

Vegetable Kabobs

cubed green pepper
cubed onion
cubed tomatoes

mushrooms
fat-free Italian dressing

Marinate first four ingredients in dressing. Skewer and grill.

Joyce Witherington Mattux,
Sea Island Beach Club Spa, class of 77

Mixed Vegetable Casserole

½ cup chopped onion
1 cup finely chopped celery
2 tablespoons margarine
1 cup light mayonnaise
1½ teaspoons curry powder

1 (32 ounce) package frozen
    mixed vegetables, thawed
approximately 2 cups oyster crackers
    or crumbled salted crackers

Sauté onion and celery in butter in microwave until tender. Mix all ingredients and spoon into greased casserole dish. Top with crumbled crackers. Bake at 350 for 35 minutes.

Yield: 6-8 servings

Janet Carson Ricciarelli

Broccoli and Cheese Casserole

4	tablespoons butter or margarine	2	boxes frozen broccoli, thawed in microwave
½	cup water		
2	tablespoons flour	3	eggs, slightly beaten
onion powder to taste		corn flake crumbs	
8	ounce jar processed cheese		

In saucepan, melt butter. In separate bowl, combine water and flour until dissolved. Add to butter and stir over medium heat until thickened. Stir in onion powder, cheese and broccoli. Stir in eggs then pour into greased casserole. Top with corn flake crumbs. Bake at 350 30-45 minutes. Freezes and microwaves well.

Yield: 8-10 servings

Susan King

Desserts

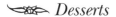

Angel Food Cake with Fruit

1	angel food cake	1	(16 ounce) container low-fat
	assorted fresh fruits (blueberries,		vanilla yogurt
	sliced strawberries, kiwi, fresh	⅓	cup honey
	peaches, peeled and diced)	⅓	cup water

Tear angel food cake into pieces about one inch square. Layer a 3 quart container with cake, then fruit, then mixture of yogurt, honey and water. Continue until finished, ending with fruit. Chill. Pretty prepared in a trifle bowl.

Yield: 12 servings

Janet Carson Ricciarelli

Banana Split Cake

2	cups crushed graham crackers	1	(medium) container frozen
1	stick margarine, softened		whipped topping, thawed
1	box powdered sugar	4	bananas
1	(8 ounce) package cream cheese,	1	small jar stemmed maraschino
	softened		cherries
1	(medium) can pineapple,	½-1	cup chopped pecans
	drained		

Mix crumbs and butter. Pat into a greased 9x13 inch pan. Beat sugar and cream cheese well. Add ¼ of thawed whipped topping and spread over crumbs. Slice bananas and arrange over cream cheese mixture. Arrange drained pineapples over this. Spread with remaining thawed whipped topping. Top with cherries and nuts. Refrigerate.

Yield: 12 servings

Pam Cunningham

Apple Butterscotch Cake

1	box yellow cake mix	1	can apple pie filling
3	eggs		

Icing:

5	tablespoons margarine	1	(12 ounce) package butterscotch
1	cup sugar		chips
⅓	cup milk		

Grease 9x13 inch pan. Mix together cake mix, eggs and pie filling. Pour into pan and bake for 30-35 minutes at 350. For icing, melt margarine. Add sugar and milk. Boil for one minute. Stir in butterscotch chips until melted. Pour over cake.

Yield: 10-12 servings

Alice Liles

Apricot Cake

2	cups sugar	2	small jars apricot baby food
4	eggs	½	cup walnuts, chopped
1	cup vegetable oil	3	ounces cream cheese, softened
2	cups flour	½	cup butter, softened
2	teaspoons baking soda	½	box powdered sugar
½	teaspoon salt		pinch salt
1½	teaspoons cinnamon	1	teaspoon vanilla

Mix sugar, eggs and oil. Add flour, baking soda, salt and cinnamon. Then add apricot baby food and walnuts. Pour into 3 greased 9 inch cake pans or a 9x13 inch pan. Bake at 350 for 40-45 minutes. Cream the cream cheese and butter. Add powdered sugar, salt and vanilla. Ice cooled cake with this cream cheese icing.

Yield: 10-12 servings

Carole Cameron

Blackberry Wine Cake

1	box pudding recipe cake mix	1	pinch salt
1	small box blackberry jello	4	eggs
1	cup oil	1	cup blackberry wine

Topping:

4	tablespoons blackberry wine	1	cup powdered sugar

Mix all cake ingredients together. Pour into lightly greased and floured Bundt pan. Bake 45 minutes at 350. While cake is baking, prepare topping by combining the topping ingredients. Pour topping over warm cake, in the pan. Remove from Bundt pan when cool.

Sharon Seawell

Simple Cinnamon Cake

2	cups flour	1	egg
pinch nutmeg		1	cup milk
pinch mace		¼	cup butter, melted
1	cup sugar	½	cup sugar
½	teaspoon salt	1	teaspoon cinnamon
2	teaspoons baking powder	powdered sugar, optional	
½	cup butter		

Mix first six ingredients. Add butter and using pastry blender, cut into dry ingredients. Bring to pebbly consistency. Add egg and milk. Mix well. Will be lumpy. Pour into greased 9x13 inch cake pan. Drip melted butter over top of batter, spreading evenly. Stir ½ cup sugar and cinnamon together and sprinkle over butter. Bake at 350 for 30 minutes. Sprinkle with powdered sugar if desired.

Yield: 12 servings

Margaret King, mother of Mark King

Blueberry Coffee Cake

Cake layer:

1	cup flour
1	teaspoon baking powder
½	teaspoon baking soda
¼	teaspoon salt
1	stick margarine, softened

⅔	cup packed light brown sugar
1	egg
¼	cup buttermilk or ¼ cup milk plus ¾ teaspoon vinegar
1	teaspoon vanilla

Topping and filling:

¼	cup flour
1	teaspoon cinnamon
3	tablespoons butter, cut into pieces

3	cups blueberries
2	teaspoons confectioners' sugar

In medium bowl, stir together flour, baking powder, baking soda and salt. In a large bowl, cream butter and sugar. Add egg, buttermilk and vanilla. Beat. Gradually add dry ingredients, beating well after each addition. Spread in an 8 inch round cake pan which has been buttered, lined with buttered wax paper, then floured. In small bowl, mix flour and cinnamon. Using pastry blender, cut in butter until mixture resembles coarse crumbs. Spread blueberries evenly over cake layer, then sprinkle with the crumb topping. Bake at 350 for 1 hour and 10 minutes or until topping is golden. Let cake cool in pan 30 minutes. Run tip of knife around the edge of pan to loosen cake. Turn onto plate. Dust with confectioners' sugar and serve warm.

Leraine Collier

Sour Cream Coconut Cake

1	box yellow cake mix
1	(12 ounce) container sour cream
12	ounces frozen coconut

2	cups sugar
1	medium container nondairy whipped topping

Bake cake according to package directions. Cool. Split each layer in half. Prepare filling by mixing sour cream, coconut and sugar. Refrigerate overnight. Reserve 1 cup filling. Spread remaining filling between layers. Combine reserved filling with whipped topping and spread on cake. Refrigerate 3-6 days before serving.

Beth Sanderson

Monkey Cake

4	cans refrigerated biscuits	1	stick butter
	sugar and cinnamon mixture	½	cup chopped nuts

Quarter each biscuit and roll in cinnamon and sugar mixture. Drop into Bundt pan. After each can of biscuits, sprinkle with nuts and a couple of teaspoons sugar and cinnamon mixture. Continue until all biscuits are rolled in sugar and cinnamon and are in Bundt pan. Melt butter in small saucepan. Add 1 cup sugar. Leftover sugar and cinnamon may be used. Bring to a full boil. Pour over biscuits. Bake at 350 45-60 minutes or until browned. Invert immediately. This reheats well in microwave, but seldom occurs since the cake "gets gone" within two hours after baking!

Susan King

Carrot Cake

4	eggs	2	teaspoons soda
1¼	cups sugar	2	teaspoons cinnamon
1	cup oil	1	teaspoon baking powder
1	teaspoon vanilla	1½	teaspoons salt
2	cups all purpose flour	2	large sized jars carrot baby food

Icing:

1	stick margarine	1	teaspoon milk
8	ounces cream cheese	¾	box 10x sugar
1	teaspoon vanilla	1	cup pecans, chopped

Beat first four ingredients. Sift together remaining ingredients, except baby food. Combine sugar and flour mixtures. Fold in baby food. Bake at 350 for 9 inch pans 25-30 minutes, 325 for 3-8 inch pans for 30 minutes. Prepare icing by creaming listed ingredients.

Elaine Clark Taylor

Quick Caramel Coffee Ring

½ cup margarine	2 tablespoons water
½ cup finely chopped nuts	2 (10 ounce) cans refrigerated
1 cup firmly packed brown sugar	flaky biscuits

In small saucepan, melt margarine. Coat bottom and sides of tube pan with 2 tablespoons melted margarine. Sprinkle 3 tablespoons of nuts on bottom of pan. Take remaining nuts, brown sugar and water and add to margarine. Heat to boiling, stirring occasionally. Remove from heat. Separate biscuits into twenty biscuits. Cut each biscuit in half and shape into a ball. Place twenty balls in bottom of pan. Drizzle ½ sauce over balls. Repeat with remaining balls. Bake at 375 for 20-25 minutes or until browned. Invert immediately onto waxed paper.

14 Carat Cake

1⅓ cups flour (2)	3 eggs (4)
1⅓ teaspoons baking powder (2)	1⅓ cups grated carrots (2)
⅔ teaspoon salt (1)	6 ounces crushed pineapple,
1⅓ teaspoons cinnamon (2)	drained (8½)
1 teaspoon soda (1½)	⅔ cup chopped nuts (1)
1⅓ cups sugar (2)	
1 cup oil (1½)	

Icing:

½ cup butter	1 box 4x sugar
8 ounces cream cheese, softened	milk
1 teaspoon vanilla	

Sift together flour, powder, salt, cinnamon and soda. Add sugar, oil and eggs. Mix well and add carrots, pineapple and nuts. Pour into 2 (or 3) greased and floured 9 inch cake pans. Bake at 350 for 35-40 minutes. Cool for a few minutes in pans, then turn out onto racks. Cool. For icing, cream butter, cream cheese and vanilla. Beat in sugar. Add a little milk if too thick. Frost cake and serve. For a three layer cake, use ingredient amounts listed ( ).

Yield: 10-12 servings

Hudock Family

Piña Colada Cake

1 package yellow cake mix	1 small can crushed pineapple,
1 can sweetened condensed milk	undrained
1 can cream of coconut	8 ounces frozen whipped topping
2 packages fresh frozen coconut	

Bake cake according to directions in a 9x13 inch pan. Remove cake from oven and punch holes in it with the handle of a wooden spoon. Immediately pour over cake a mixture of one package of the fresh frozen coconut and the condensed milk. Let this soak in, then spread the can of undrained pineapple over the top. Mix the remaining coconut with the whipped topping and spread over the cooled cake. Cover and refrigerate for 24 hours before serving. For a pretty Christmas cake, decorate this with red cherries.

Yield: 16-18 servings

Jill Gravely

Pineapple Cake

20 ounce can crushed pineapple,	2 eggs
undrained	2 teaspoons baking powder
2 cups flour	1 cup chopped nuts
2 cups sugar	

Frosting:

8 ounces cream cheese, softened	1½ cups powdered sugar
1 stick butter, softened	1 teaspoon vanilla

Combine all cake ingredients in a large bowl and mix well. Pour into a greased and floured 9x13 inch pan. Bake at 300 for one hour. Cool. Cream together all icing ingredients and frost cooled cake.

Erma Auer

The Best Pineapple Cake

1   box yellow cake, baked in round
    pans according to directions
    and cooled

Filling:

1 cup water	2 tablespoons flour (about)
2 cups sugar	water
1 large can crushed pineapple	1 teaspoon vanilla

Icing:

1 stick margarine, softened	8 ounces cream cheese, softened
¼ cup milk	1 box 10x confectioners' sugar

Mix water and sugar in saucepan. Boil 5 minutes. Add pineapple and boil an additional 5 minutes. Add flour mixed with enough water to moisten. Let thicken. Add vanilla. Set aside. Mix icing ingredients together. Slice cake into thin layers. Spread pineapple filling on first layer, then spread icing over pineapple filling. Repeat each layer the same, ending with icing.

Yield: 12-16 servings

Strawberry Cake

1 box white cake mix	4 eggs
1 (3½ ounce) box strawberry jello	1 cup strawberries
1 cup oil	1 cup nuts
½ cup milk	1 cup flaked coconut

Icing:

1 box confectioners' sugar	½ cup nuts
1 stick butter	½ cup flaked coconut
½ cup strawberries	

Mix cake mix, jello, oil, milk and eggs. Bake in a 9x13 inch pan at 350 for 35 minutes. Mix icing ingredients and spread over warm cake. Cool and refrigerate.

Yield: 12 servings

Betty Lou Trimboli

Lemon Poppy Seed Cake

1	box yellow cake mix	¼	jar poppy seeds
1	(3½ ounce) box instant vanilla pudding	½	cup vegetable oil
		4	eggs
1	(3½ ounce) box instant lemon pudding	1	cup hot water

Mix all ingredients about four minutes. Spray three small loaf pans and evenly fill with batter. Bake at 350 approximately 50 minutes or until cake is done.

Jill Gravely

Chocolate Chip Pound Cake

1	box yellow cake mix	¾	cup water
1	(3½ ounce) package vanilla instant pudding	½	cup oil
		8	ounces sour cream
2	eggs	1	(6 ounce) bag chocolate chips

Mix ingredients and pour into a greased Bundt pan. Bake for one hour at 325.

Yield: 12 servings

Joan Braswell

Lemon Pound Cake

1	box moist yellow cake mix	⅔	cup cold water
1	(4 ounce) box jello instant lemon pie filling	2	teaspoons lemon extract
⅔	cup vegetable oil	4	eggs

Glaze:

2	cups sifted powdered sugar	juice of two lemons

Mix cake ingredients and bake at 325 for 40 minutes. Cool. Pour glaze over cake.

Crystal Wooten

Golden Amaretto Cake

1 (18½ ounce) package yellow cake mix	¾ cup plus 6 tablespoons Amaretto, divided
½ cup vegetable oil	½ cup water
1 (6 ounce) package instant vanilla pudding	¼ teaspoon almond extract
4 eggs	1 cup confectioners' sugar

In a bowl, blend cake mix, oil, pudding, eggs, ¾ cup Amaretto, water and almond extract. Pour into a well-greased, lightly floured Bundt pan. Bake cake at 350 for 40-45 minutes or until cake springs back when lightly touched. In a small bowl, stir together 6 teaspoons Amaretto and sugar. Poke holes in warm cake with skewer and pour glaze over top. Cool cake in pan 2 hours.

Yield: 12 servings

Lisa Williams Merriam, class of 78

Buttermilk Pound Cake

3 cups sugar	3 cups flour
½ cup vegetable shortening	1 cup buttermilk
½ cup butter	½ teaspoon baking soda dissolved in 1 tablespoon water
5 whole eggs	2 teaspoons vanilla
½ teaspoon salt	

Cream together sugar, shortening and butter. Add eggs, one at a time, and beat well. Combine salt and flour. Combine buttermilk and soda mix. To the creamed mixture, alternately add the flour mix and the buttermilk mix, beating well each time. Blend in vanilla. Pour into a greased and floured Bundt pan. Bake at 300 for 1 hour and 15 minutes.

Yield: 12 servings

Trish Dozier

191

Cream Cheese Pound Cake

1   (8 ounce) package cream cheese, softened
3   sticks margarine or butter, softened
3   cups sugar

1   tablespoon vanilla
6   eggs
3   cups cake flour
½   teaspoon salt
¼   teaspoon soda

Beat cream cheese until fluffy. Add margarine or butter. Beat until fluffy. Add sugar and vanilla. Add eggs one at a time, beating after each addition. Combine flour, salt and soda. Slowly add, one cup at a time. Pour into greased and floured 10 inch tube pan or two 9 inch loaf pans. Bake at 350 for 45-60 minutes. For variation add 4 squares unsweetened chocolate, melted, to the butter and cream cheese mixture.

Yield: 12 servings

Judy Grant

Chocolate Cherry Cake

1   box chocolate cake mix
3   eggs

1   can cherry pie filling

Icing:

1   cup sugar
5   tablespoons margarine
⅓   cup milk

1   (12 ounce) package chocolate chips

Mix together cake mix, eggs and pie filling. Pour into greased 9x13 inch pan and bake at 350 for 30-35 minutes. Melt margarine. Add sugar and milk. Boil one minute. Stir in chocolate chips until melted. Pour over cake.

Yield: 10-12 servings

Alice Liles

Chocolate Fudge Cake

1 stick margarine	1 teaspoon baking powder
1 cup sugar	1 teaspoon vanilla
4 eggs	1 (16 ounce) can chocolate syrup
1 cup plain flour	

Icing:

1 stick margarine	6 ounces chocolate chips
1/3 cup evaporated milk	1/2 cup chopped pecans
1 cup sugar	

Mix all ingredients together and pour into greased 10x14 inch pan. Bake at 350 for 40-45 minutes.

Mix first three icing ingredients and cook 2 minutes at boiling point. Remove from heat and add chocolate chips and chopped pecans. Pour on cake immediately after you remove it from the oven. Do not let the cake cool.

Chocolate Raspberry Cake

1 box butter recipe chocolate cake mix	1/2 cup seedless raspberry jam
1 (12 ounce) package semi-sweet chocolate chips	1 (8 ounce) container sour cream
1/4 cup raspberry liqueur	2 tablespoons toasted chopped pecans

Prepare cake mix according to directions. Stir in 1 cup chocolate chips. Bake in two round pans according to package directions. Cool and remove from pans. Brush cake tops with raspberry liqueur. Spread jam on the bottom layer. Place top layer on top of jam. Melt remaining chocolate chips over low heat. Gradually stir in sour cream. Spread sour cream frosting on top and sides of cake. Sprinkle top with toasted pecans. Chill cake for two hours.

Yield: 12 servings

Trish Dozier

193

Chocolate Pound Cake

½	cup vegetable shortening	3	cups plain flour
2	sticks butter	½	teaspoon baking powder
3	cups sugar	1	teaspoon salt
5	eggs	1	cup milk
5	tablespoons cocoa	1	teaspoon vanilla

Cream vegetable shortening, butter and sugar. Add eggs, one at a time. Add cocoa. Add rest of dry ingredients alternately with milk. Add vanilla. Bake at 325 for 1 hour and 25 minutes.

Beth Sanderson

Chocolate Picnic Cake

2	cups flour	5	tablespoons cocoa
2	cups sugar	½	cup buttermilk
1	cup water	2	eggs
½	cup margarine	1	teaspoon baking soda
½	cup shortening	1	teaspoon vanilla

Frosting:

½	cup margarine	1	(16 ounce) box powdered sugar
6	tablespoons milk	1	teaspoon vanilla
4	tablespoons cocoa	1	cup chopped nuts

Sift together flour and sugar. In a saucepan, cook water, margarine, shortening and cocoa until melted. Cool. Pour over the flour mixture and mix well. Add buttermilk, eggs, soda and vanilla. Mix well. Pour into a greased 9x13 inch pan and bake at 350 for 25-35 minutes. For frosting, bring margarine, milk and cocoa to a boil. Remove from heat and add sugar, vanilla and nuts. Pour over hot cake and leave cake in the pan.

Yield: 12 servings

Lisa Hines

Hot Fudge Cake

1 cup all purpose flour	2 tablespoons vegetable oil
¾ cup sugar	1 teaspoon vanilla extract
6 tablespoons cocoa, divided	1 cup packed brown sugar
2 teaspoons baking powder	1¾ cups hot water
¼ teaspoon salt	whipped cream or ice cream
½ cup milk	(optional)

In a medium bowl, combine flour, sugar, 2 tablespoons cocoa, baking powder and salt. Stir in milk, oil and vanilla until smooth. Spread in an ungreased 9 inch square baking pan. Combine brown sugar and remaining cocoa. Sprinkle over batter. Pour hot water over all. Do not stir. Bake at 350 for 35-40 minutes. Serve warm. Top with whipped or ice cream if desired.

Yield: 9 servings

Barbara Rose

Hot Fudge Cake

1 cup self-rising flour	½ cup milk
¾ cup sugar	1 teaspoon vanilla
2 tablespoons cocoa	2 tablespoons butter, melted
⅛ teaspoon salt	½ cup chopped nuts (optional)

Sauce:

½ cup sugar	5 tablespoons cocoa
½ cup brown sugar	1 cup hot water

Sift dry ingredients for cake. Add milk and stir. Add vanilla, butter and nuts. Stir until smooth. Pour into a greased 9x9 inch pan. Mix ingredients for sauce and pour over cake. Bake at 350 for 30 minutes. Serve warm.

Yield: 10 servings

Betty Lou Trimboli

Coffee-Toffee Ice Cream Cake

28 chocolate sandwich cookies
6 large chocolate covered toffee
  bars

½ gallon chocolate ice cream,
  softened
½ gallon coffee ice cream, softened
8 ounces chocolate syrup

Put 14 cookies in each of two plastic bags. Crush cookies. Do not use food processor. Place candy toffee bars in a plastic bag and crush. Lightly oil a ten inch springform pan. Sprinkle bottom of pan with one bag of crushed cookies. Add ½ gallon of chocolate ice cream. Drizzle 4 ounces of chocolate syrup over ice cream. Sprinkle remaining bag of cookies over syrup. Add ½ gallon coffee ice cream. Drizzle 4 ounces chocolate syrup over ice cream. Sprinkle toffee candy over the top, cover with foil and freeze.

Yield: 25 servings

Kathy Sawyer

Summer Cake

1 package butter golden cake mix
½ cup butter or margarine
½ cup oil

4 eggs
1 (11 ounce) can mandarin
  oranges

Icing:
1 (12 ounce) container frozen
  whipped topping
1 (21 ounce) can crushed
  pineapple, undrained

1 (3½ ounce) package instant
  vanilla pudding

In a large mixing bowl, put cake mix, butter, oil and eggs. Drain the liquid from the oranges into the bowl of ingredients. Mix for 3 minutes with mixer. Fold in oranges. Grease and flour 3 nine inch round cake pans. Pour batter into pans and bake at 375 for 20-25 minutes. For icing, mix whipped topping, pineapple and pudding mix until smooth. Spread between layers of cake, then on top and sides.

Yield: 12 servings

Linda Haven

Rum Cake

1	box yellow cake mix	½	cup chopped pecans
1	box instant pudding mix	1	stick margarine
4	eggs, slightly beaten	1	cup sugar
½	cup salad oil	¼	cup water
½	cup water	¼	cup rum
½	cup light rum		

Mix first six ingredients. Place pecans in bottom of tube pan. Pour cake mixture over nuts. Bake at 325 for 50-60 minutes or until cake tester is clean. Remove from oven and cool 20 minutes. Remove from pan. Make glaze by bringing remaining ingredients to a boil for 2-3 minutes, stirring constantly. With cake tester, prick top of cake 10-20 times. Pour hot glaze over cake.

Rum Cake

1	cup chopped nuts	½	cup water
1	box yellow cake mix	½	cup oil
1	(3½ ounce) box instant vanilla pudding	½	cup rum (light or dark)

Syrup:

1	cup sugar	½	cup butter
¼	cup water	3	ounces rum

Spray a Bundt pan with spray oil. Sprinkle nuts on bottom of pan. Mix all of the remaining cake ingredients and pour into pan. Bake at 325 for one hour. Just before cake is done, prepare syrup by heating sugar, water, butter and rum in small pan. Pour over hot cake, still in pan. Cool cake completely.

Yield: 12 servings

Cathy Green

Turtle Cake

1   box German chocolate cake mix
1   bag caramels
1   (5 ounce) can evaporated milk
6   ounces chocolate chips
1   cup chopped nuts

Prepare cake mix according to directions. Pour ½ cake mixture into greased 9x13 inch pan. Bake 20 minutes. Combine caramels and canned milk over medium heat, stirring until melted. Pour ¾ caramel mixture over cake. Sprinkle 4 ounces chocolate chips and ¾ cup nuts over caramel. Next pour remaining cake batter on top and sprinkle with remaining chocolate chips and nuts. Bake an additional 30-40 minutes. Remove cake and immediately pour remaining caramel mixture on top.

Yield: 10 servings

Kay Allen Blizzard, class of 74

Frozen Mocha Cheesecake

1¼ cups chocolate wafer cookie
    crumbs (approximately 24
    cookies)
¼   cup margarine, melted
¼   cup sugar
1   (8 ounce) package cream cheese,
    softened
1   (14 ounce) can sweetened
    condensed milk
⅔   cup chocolate syrup
1-2 tablespoons instant coffee
    (optional)
1   teaspoon hot water
½   pint whipping cream, whipped
    or 1 cup frozen whipped topping

Combine crumbs, margarine and sugar. Press firmly into bottom and sides of 8-9 inch springform pan or 9x13 inch baking dish. In large mixing bowl, beat cheese until fluffy. Gradually beat in sweetened condensed milk and chocolate syrup until smooth. In small bowl, dissolve coffee in water. Add to cheese mixture. Mix well. Fold in whipping cream or frozen whipped topping. Pour into prepared pan. Freeze 6 hours or overnight. Garnish with chocolate crumbs if desired. Return leftovers to freezer.

Yield: 8-12 servings

Janet Carson Ricciarelli

Chocolate Snaps and Whip Cream

½ cup sugar
½ cup whipping cream

4 boxes chocolate snaps (chocolate teddy grahams may be substituted)

Whip cream with mixer and add sugar while mixing. Layer chocolate snaps, then whipped cream. Start with chocolate snaps and end with chocolate snaps. Prepare day ahead to soften snaps. Refrigerate.

Yield: 4 servings

Jennifer Heath Sutton, class of 90

Heath Bar Cake

1 angel food cake
1 large container nondairy whipped topping

5-6 chocolate covered toffee bars, crushed
4 tablespoons cocoa

Cut a round angel food cake into two layers. Mix together remaining ingredients to make icing, saving a small amount of crushed candy for garnish. Ice bottom layer. Place second layer on top and ice top and sides. Garnish with remaining crushed candy.

Yield: 12 servings

Christian Cherry, class of 95

No-Bake Cheesecake

1 (8 ounce) package cream cheese at room temperature
1 (14 ounce) can sweetened condensed milk

⅓ cup fresh lemon juice
1 teaspoon vanilla
1 graham cracker crust

Beat cheese until fluffy. Add milk, lemon juice and vanilla. Mix well. Pour into pie shell. Refrigerate 3 hours.

Yield: 6-8 servings

Crystal Wooten

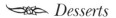

Pumpkin Spice Cake

1 box spice cake mix	1 can pumpkin pie filling
3 eggs	

Icing:

1 cup sugar	1 (12 ounce) package butterscotch
5 tablespoons margarine	chips
⅓ cup milk	

Mix together cake mix, eggs and pie filling. Pour into greased 9x13 inch pan and bake at 350 for 30-35 minutes. For icing, melt margarine. Add sugar and milk. Boil for one minute. Stir in chips and stir until melted. Pour over cake.

Yield: 10-12 servings

Alice Liles

Chocolate Amaretto Cheesecake

vegetable cooking spray	2 cups sugar
½ cup teddy bear shaped chocolate graham cookie crumbs, divided	⅔ cup all purpose flour
	2 tablespoons vanilla extract
4 (8 ounce) packages cream cheese, fat free	½ cup egg substitute
	whipped cream and sliced almonds
⅔ cup unsweetened cocoa	for garnish
3 tablespoons Amaretto	

Sprinkle ¼ cup crumbs on bottom of a 9 inch springform pan coated with cooking spray. Set remaining ¼ cup crumbs aside. Position knife blade in food processor bowl. Add cream cheese, cocoa, Amaretto, sugar, flour and vanilla. Process until smooth. Add egg substitute and process just until blended. Pour mixture into pan. Bake at 300 for 45-50 minutes or until center is almost set. Sprinkle with remaining crumbs. Let cool completely on a wire rack. Cover and refrigerate 8 hours. Top each slice with a small amount of whipped cream and sprinkle with sliced almonds. 226 calories, 2.1 grams fat

Yield: 16 servings

Joyce Witherington Mattux,
Sea Isalnd Beach Club Spa, class of 77

Cheesecake

4	(8 ounce) packages cream cheese	1¼	cups sugar
1	(16 ounce) container sour cream	2	tablespoons cornstarch
		2	teaspoons vanilla
½	cup evaporated milk	5	eggs

Let cream cheese, sour cream, milk and eggs stand at room temperature for at least one hour. Blend cream cheese, sour cream and milk. Add sugar, cornstarch and vanilla. Beat on high until well blended. Beat in eggs, one at a time. Continue beating until mixture is very smooth. Grease and flour a 9 or 10 inch spring form cheesecake pan. Cover bottom of pan coming up the sides with aluminum foil to make it water tight. Place pan in a large roasting pan filled with enough warm water to come half way up the side of the cake pan. Bake at 350 for one hour. Turn oven off and leave cake in with oven door open for another hour.

Banana Split Pie

2	cups graham cracker crumbs	6-8	bananas
1	stick margarine, melted	1	small can crushed pineapple, drained
3	cups powdered sugar		
1	(8 ounce) package cream cheese, softened	1	(16 ounce) container frozen whipped topping
1	egg	½	cup finely chopped pecans

Mix graham cracker crumbs and margarine and form into a crust in a 9x12 inch dish. Mix sugar, cream cheese and egg. Beat well. Pour creamed mixture on top of crust. Slice bananas long ways and layer on top of pie. Spread pineapple on bananas. Spread whipped topping over pineapple. Sprinkle with nuts. Refrigerate.

Yield: 12 servings

Cindy Beaman

Refrigerator Blueberry Banana Pie

1	baked pie shell, cooled	1	pint blueberries
1	(6 ounce) package cream cheese, softened	2	tablespoons flour
		¾	cup sugar
sugar to taste		1	(8 ounce) container frozen
1	banana, sliced		whipped topping

Mix cream cheese and sugar to taste. Spread mixture on the bottom of pie crust. Cover cream cheese with sliced banana. In a medium saucepan, combine blueberries, flour and ¾ cup sugar. Cook over medium heat until sugar dissolves. Pour cooked blueberries over bananas. Spread frozen whipped topping over blueberries. Refrigerate.

Yield: 8 servings

Jean Jones

Frozen Lemon Pie

1½	cups graham cracker crumbs	½	cup lemon juice
½	cup sugar	8	ounce container frozen whipped
1	stick butter, melted		topping
2	cans sweetened condensed milk		

Combine crumbs and sugar in pie plate. Add butter and mix well. Press into a crust. Bake 5 minutes or until set. Combine milk and lemon juice. Stir until smooth. Pour into pie crust. Spread frozen whipped topping over pie. Freeze at least overnight. Let stand at room temperature 30 minutes before serving. This pie can be prepared well in advance. The longer it freezes, the better it tastes.

Yield: 6-8 servings

Paige Smith Hutto, class of 89

Buttermilk Pie

2 cups sugar	1 cup buttermilk
3 tablespoons flour	3 eggs, beaten
⅔ cup butter, melted	2 frozen prepared pie crusts
1 teaspoon vanilla	

Mix together sugar and flour. Add remaining ingredients and mix well. Pour mixture into pie crusts. Bake at 325 for 45 minutes. Makes two pies.

Yield: 16 servings

Nancy Bowers

Cherry Pie

2 (8 ounce) packages cream cheese at room temperature	2 (15 ounce) cans cherry pie filling
1 can sweetened condensed milk	vanilla to taste
⅓ cup lemon juice	2 graham cracker crusts

Beat cheese until fluffy. Add milk, lemon juice and vanilla. Mix well. Pour into crusts. Chill to firm. Place cherry pie filling on top.

Yield: 10-12 servings

Leraine Collier

No Crust Coconut Pie

½ cup self rising flour	2 cups milk
1¾ cups sugar	1 teaspoon vanilla
½ stick margarine, melted	6 ounces grated coconut
4 eggs, well beaten	

Mix flour and sugar in a bowl. Add the margarine, eggs, milk, vanilla and coconut. Mix well. Pour into two ungreased aluminum pie plates. Bake at 350 for 35 minutes or until light and brown.

Yield: 8 servings

Sharlene Vainright

203

Grandma Bet's Lemon Custard Pie

2   cups sugar
2   tablespoons cornmeal
1   tablespoon flour
4   eggs, unbeaten
¼   cup butter, melted

¼   cup milk
¼   cup lemon juice
4   teaspoons grated lemon rind
2   unbaked pie shells

Mix sugar, cornmeal and flour. Add eggs, one at a time beating well after each. Stir in butter, milk, lemon juice and rind. Mix well. Pour mixture into two unbaked pie shells. Bake at 350 for 45 minutes or until firm.

Yield: 16 servings

Sarah Exum Edwards

Sly Lemon Pie

1   quart vanilla low-fat or no-fat frozen yogurt or ice cream, softened
6   ounces frozen lemonade concentrate, thawed

1   9 inch graham cracker crust pie shell
½   pint heavy cream, whipped (for garnish - optional)
sliced lemon twists (for garnish - optional)

Combine softened (not melted) frozen yogurt and lemonade in a bowl and stir until smooth. Pour into pie shell. Freeze until firm, about 1½ hours. Let stand about 10 minutes before serving. Garnish with whipped cream and lemon twists if desired.

Yield: 6-8 servings

Linda Peacock

Frozen Lemonade Pie

1   (14 ounce) can sweetened
    condensed milk
1   (6 ounce) can frozen lemonade
    concentrate, thawed and
    undiluted

1   (8 ounce) container frozen
    whipped topping, thawed
2   (9 inch) prepared graham
    cracker crusts

Fold milk and lemonade concentrate into whipped topping. Spoon into crusts. Freeze until firm. Remove from freezer about 30 minutes before serving. Makes two pies.

Yield: 12-16 servings

Elizabeth Hood

Easy, Low Fat Key Lime Pie

1   reduced fat graham cracker
    crust
1   container fat-free nondairy
    whipped topping

1   can fat-free sweetened condensed
    milk
1   package lemon-lime drink mix

Mix all ingredients, except crust. Pour into crust and chill. Delicious!

Vicki Waters Downing, class of 80

Lydia's Key Lime Pie

4   egg whites
3   ounces lime juice
1   can lite sweetened condensed
    milk

1   graham cracker crust
8   ounces whipped topping for
    frosting

Stir all ingredients except for crust. Pour into crust. Bake at 350 for 30 minutes. Cool. Frost with whipped topping or whipped cream. Refrigerate and serve cold.

Yield: 8 servings

Frances Parrott

Chocolate Chip Lime Pie

1 (14 ounce) can sweetened condensed milk
1 (6 ounce) frozen limeade concentrate, thawed and undiluted
½ cup lime juice

3-4 drops green food coloring
1 (6 ounce) bag semi-sweet chocolate chips
2 (8 ounce) containers of frozen whipped topping, thawed
2 (6 ounce) flavored crumb crusts

Combine all ingredients except crusts, reserving a few chips for garnish. Mix well with electric mixer. Pour mixture into pie crusts and garnish with chips or chocolate curls. Freeze.

Yield: 8 servings

Lee Adams

Martian Pie

1 package pistachio pudding
1 (15 ounce) can pineapple in own juice

1 small container frozen whipped topping
1 graham cracker pie crust (chocolate is great)

Combine first three ingredients. Fold into pie shell. Place in freezer for 20 minutes or until firm.

Sandra Warren

Chocolate Pie

1 cup sugar
1 tablespoon flour
1 tablespoon butter
1 tablespoon vanilla
2 eggs
1 cup milk

2 tablespoons cocoa
baked pie shell
6 egg whites
½ teaspoon cream of tartar
6 tablespoons sugar

Mix first seven ingredients together over low heat until stiff. Pour into baked pie shell. Make meringue by beating remaining ingredients until stiff.

Betty Lou Waters

206

Swedish Meringue Pie

3	egg whites	½	teaspoon baking powder
¼	teaspoon cream of tartar	1	cup chopped pecans
1	teaspoon vanilla	8	ounces frozen whipped topping,
1	cup sugar		thawed
20	crushed butter crackers		

Whip egg whites, cream of tartar and vanilla until stiff peaks form. Gradually add sugar and beat until mixed. Into the egg mixture fold the crackers, baking powder and pecans. Pour into a greased pie plate and bake at 325 for 30-40 minutes. Refrigerate 24 hours before serving. Top with whipped topping.

Yield: 6 servings

Jean Jones

Chocolate Seduction Pie

1	(10 inch) frozen deep dish pie shell, unbaked	½	cup half and half
2	sticks butter	4	eggs at room temperature
5	ounces unsweetened chocolate	1	egg yolk
2½	cups sugar	1½	teaspoons vanilla

Bake pie shell for 5 minutes at 400. Reduce oven temperature to 350. Melt butter and chocolate in top of a double boiler over gently simmering water, stirring frequently. Add sugar and half and half. Stir until sugar dissolves and mixture is smooth. In a small bowl, beat eggs and egg yolk. Gradually add eggs to chocolate, stirring until thick and smooth. Blend in vanilla. Pour into crust and bake until set, about 35 minutes.

Yield: 10 servings

Trish Dozier

French Silk Pie

3	egg whites	1	(4 ounce) package sweet baking
⅛	teaspoon salt		chocolate
¼	teaspoon cream of tartar	3	tablespoons water
¾	cup sugar	1	tablespoon brandy
½	cup chopped pecans or walnuts	2	cups heavy cream, divided
½	teaspoon vanilla extract		

In a bowl, blend egg whites until foamy. Add salt and cream of tartar. Add sugar gradually and continue beating until stiff peaks form. Fold in nuts and vanilla. Spoon into pie pan, forming a next by building up a half inch rim around the edge. Bake at 300 for 50 minutes. Cool. In a double boiler, melt chocolate and water. Cool. Add brandy to the chocolate mixture. Whip 1 cup of the cream and fold into the chocolate mixture. Spoon into meringue shell and chill 2-3 hours. Before serving, whip remaining 1 cup of cream and top the pie. Garnish with chocolate curls.

Yield: 8 servings

Nancy Bowers

Date Skillet Cookies

1	stick margarine	1	teaspoon vanilla
¾	cup sugar	1	cup pecans, chopped finely
2	egg yolks	2	cups crispy rice cereal
½	pound chopped dates	1	can flake coconut

Melt margarine in skillet. Add sugar, eggs, yolks and dates, constantly mashing dates. Stir while cooking over low heat. Cook approximately 10 minutes. Remove from burner and add vanilla, nuts and rice cereal. As soon as possible start making marble sized balls. Roll each one in coconut flakes. Let cool on wax paper. Store in airtight container.

T. A. Smith's Great-great Grandmother Richardson

Double Layer Chocolate Pie

4 ounces cream cheese, softened	1 pie crust, baked and cooled
1 tablespoon milk	2 cups cold milk
1 tablespoon sugar	2 (4 serving size) packages
1 (8 ounce) container frozen	chocolate pudding
whipped topping, thawed	

Mix cream cheese, milk and sugar until smooth. Stir in half of the frozen whipped topping. Spread on bottom of the crust. Mix pudding and milk. Stir in remaining whipped topping. Spread over cream cheese layer. Refrigerate.

Dina Trimboli Whitley, class of 80

Fudge Pie

½ cup margarine, melted	¼ teaspoon vanilla
¼ cup cocoa	2 eggs
¼ cup flour	pecans, if desired
1 cup sugar	

Mix all ingredients and pour into a pie pan. Bake at 350 for 25 minutes.

Yield: 6 servings

Jenette Low

Brownies

2 cups sugar	3 eggs
2 sticks margarine, melted	½ teaspoon vanilla
½ cup cocoa	1½ cups flour, sifted

Mix sugar, margarine, cocoa, eggs and vanilla until blended. Add flour. Stir until lumps disappear. Bake at 350 on top rack for 30-35 minutes.

Christian Cherry, class of 95

Decadent Brownie

1   box brownie mix with fudge
    packet
½   cup chocolate chips
chocolate syrup

1   pint fresh raspberries
raspberry preserves
8   ounces whipped topping

Bake brownie mix as directed on box, adding chocolate chips. Cool. Spread a small amount of preserves on a dessert plate. Place brownie on plate. Drizzle chocolate syrup on brownie. Top with whipped topping and fresh raspberries.

Kathy White

Butterscotch Brownies

1   (16 ounce) box dark brown
    sugar
2   sticks margarine, softened
4   eggs

1¾ cups self-rising flour
12 ounces butterscotch chips
pecans, optional

Blend sugar, margarine and eggs. Add flour until well mixed. Turn into greased 10x14 inch pan. Top with butterscotch chips and nuts. Bake at 350 for 25 minutes. Remove and turn out of pan. Cut into squares.

Laura O'Brien

Chocolate Chip Cake Mix Cookies

1   box yellow cake mix
½   cup oil
2   tablespoons water

2   eggs
6   ounce package semi-sweet
    chocolate chips

Mix all ingredients. Drop by teaspoons on ungreased cookie sheet. Bake at 350 for 8-10 minutes or until lightly brown. For variety: lemon cake mix and rice krispies, fudge marble cake mix and coconut, spice cake mix and raisins, German chocolate cake mix with coconut and chocolate chips.

Yield: 3-4 dozen

Lee Adams

Fudge

3   cups sugar
1½   sticks margarine
small can evaporated milk
16-17 large marshmallows

12 ounces chocolate chips
1   teaspoon vanilla
1   cup chopped nuts

Boil first three ingredients 3 minutes. Stir in marshmallows until melted. Stir in remaining ingredients. Pour into buttered 9x13 inch pan.

Beth Sanderson

Other Mother's Chocolate Chip Cookies

1   box butter yellow cake mix
½   cup oil

large package chocolate chips
2   eggs

Mix all ingredients except chips. Fold in chips. Drop on ungreased cookie sheet. Bake at 100 for 5 minutes (until crisp).

Virgil Stewart, grandmother of Mary Elizabeth

Phase Banana Pudding

5   cups milk
3   packages instant vanilla
     pudding
1   teaspoon vanilla
8   ounces sour cream

1   large container nondairy
     whipped topping
1   box vanilla wafers
1   large bunch bananas (8-12)

Blend milk, pudding mix and vanilla, alternating milk and pudding until blended. Add sour cream and ½ of the whipped topping. Layer in a 9x13 inch pan beginning with vanilla wafers, then bananas, then pudding. Top with remaining whipped topping. This recipe can be cut in half if needed. This makes enough for a crowd.

Vicki Waters Downing, class of 80

Whiskey Balls

½   pound bag vanilla wafers
1   cup pecans, chopped
1   cup powdered sugar

3   tablespoons corn syrup
1½ teaspoons cocoa
2½ jiggers whiskey

Crush wafers with rolling pin. Mix sugar and cocoa and add to wafers and mix. Put rest of ingredients together then mix all together. Shape into small balls and roll in powdered sugar. Will keep 2 or 3 weeks. This is a New Orleans favorite.

Doris Gaudet

Mom's Bread Pudding

1   quart skim milk
¾ cup sugar
2   eggs
1   teaspoon vanilla

½ teaspoon salt
butter
8   slices stale bread
½-1 cup raisins

In large ovenproof bowl, combine milk, sugar, eggs, vanilla and salt. Butter bread and put into milk mixture. When soft, add raisins and bake at 350 until firm, about 1-1½ hours.

Yield: 10 servings

Joyce Gaudet Booth, mother of Susan King

Banana Pudding

2   packages instant vanilla
    pudding
3   cups milk
¾ cup sugar
8   ounces sour cream

1   small container nondairy
    whipped topping
vanilla wafers
bananas

Mix first three ingredients. Add sour cream and whipped topping. Layer vanilla wafers, bananas and pudding mixture. Refrigerate.

Beth Sanderson

Fruit Cupcakes

4 cups bread crumbs (fine)	1 teaspoon vanilla
1½ cups milk	1 teaspoon cinnamon
1 stick margarine	1 teaspoon cloves
2 eggs, slightly beaten	3 tablespoons flour for fruit
1 cup sugar	1 cup chopped pecans
1 teaspoon baking soda	1 cup dates, chopped
¾ cup molasses	2 cups raisins

Soak bread crumbs in milk 30 minutes. Add margarine, eggs and sugar. Mix well. Add baking soda to molasses then add to mixture. Add vanilla, cinnamon and cloves. Mix flour, nuts, dates and raisins. Add to mixture. Fill muffin cups ¾ full. Bake at 350 for 25-30 minutes. Store in sealed container. This is a recipe from the year 1900.

T. A. Smith's Great-great Grandmother Richardson.

Christmas Peanut Butter Balls

2 cups crisp rice cereal	1 cup butter
1 (16 ounce) box confectioners	1 (12 ounce) package chocolate
sugar	chips (butterscotch can be used)
2 cups peanut butter	

Combine cereal and sugar in a bowl. Melt peanut butter and butter. Pour over cereal and sugar. Mix until blended. Roll in ½ inch balls. Melt chocolate and roll balls in the melted chocolate. Place on wax paper to cool.

Lisa Mumford Kluttz, class of 88

Peanut Butter Creams

2 (12 ounce) packages milk
    chocolate morsels
1 can sweetened condensed milk

1½ teaspoons vanilla
½ cup chopped nuts (optional)
1 cup peanut butter

Melt morsels in pan with peanut butter. Add nuts. Remove from heat and add vanilla. Add condensed milk, remembering that mixture will harden rapidly after milk is added. Spread onto waxed paper lined baking pan or dish. Chill. Cut into squares in pan or turn onto cutting board, peel off wax paper and cut.

Linda Haven

Easy Carrot Cupcakes with Creamy Frosting

1½ cups raw carrots, finely grated
1 cup all purpose flour
¾ cup sugar
1 teaspoon cinnamon
1 teaspoon baking powder
½ teaspoon baking soda

¼ teaspoon salt
2 eggs, beaten
⅓ cup vegetable oil
¼ cup applesauce
½ teaspoon vanilla

Creamy Frosting:

1 (3 ounce) package light
    cream cheese, softened
¼ cup butter, softened

1 teaspoon vanilla
2½-2¾ cups confectioners sugar, sifted
12 pecan halves

Line 12 muffin cups with paper liners. Combine first seven ingredients in large mixing bowl. Add eggs, oil, applesauce and vanilla. Beat on medium speed for 1 minute. Fill prepared muffin cups ¾ full. Bake at 375 for 20-25 minutes. Remove from pan and cool on wire rack. For frosting, beat together cream cheese, butter and vanilla until light and fluffy. Gradually add sugar, one cup at a time, to make frosting spreading consistency. Frost cupcakes and garnish with pecan halves.

Yield: 12 servings

Linda Peacock

Butterscotch Torte

1½ sticks butter
1 cup chopped pecans
1½ cups flour
12 ounces cream cheese
1½ cups 4x sugar

1 (9 ounce) container whipped topping, thawed
2 packages instant butterscotch pudding mix
3 cups milk

Combine butter, pecans and flour to make a crust. Spread in a 9x13 inch pan. Bake at 350 for 15 minutes. Cool completely. Cream together cream cheese and 4x sugar. Spread over cooled crust. Spread 1½ cups whipped topping over cream cheese mixture. Mix pudding and milk together, then spread over the whipped topping. Top with remainder of whipped topping. Refrigerate at least 24 hours.

Yield: 12-16 servings

Karen Williams

Chocolate Torte

1 stick margarine
2 tablespoons granulated sugar
1 cup plain flour
½ cup chopped pecans
8 ounces cream cheese
1 (9 ounce) container frozen whipped topping, thawed

1½ cups powdered sugar
2 packages instant pudding (chocolate, lemon, butterscotch or coconut - ½ cup canned coconut should be added to coconut pudding)
3 cups milk

Combine margarine, sugar, flour and pecans to make a crust. Pat into a 9x13 inch pan. Bake at 350 for 15 minutes. Cool. Combine cream cheese, whipped topping and powdered sugar. Spread over cooled crust. Mix pudding and milk. Pour over cream cheese layer. Cover all with whipped topping. Garnish with appropriate flavor to enhance pudding choice.

Yield 12-16 servings

Sharlene Vainright

Fudgey Pecan Torte

1 cup butter or margarine, melted	3 tablespoons water
1½ cups sugar	¾ cup finely chopped pecans
1½ teaspoons vanilla extract	⅛ teaspoon cream of tartar
3 eggs, separated	⅛ teaspoon salt
⅔ cup cocoa	pecan halves for garnish
½ cup all purpose flour	

Royal Glaze:

1⅓ cups semi-sweet chocolate chips   ½ cup whipping cream (I have used milk)

Prepare Royal Glaze by combining, in small saucepan, chocolate chips and whipping cream or milk. Cook over low heat, stirring constantly until chips are melted and mixture begins to thicken. Set aside. Line bottom of 9 inch springform pan with aluminum foil. Butter foil and side of pan. Heat oven to 350. In large mixing bowl, combine butter, sugar and vanilla. Beat well. Add egg yolks, one at a time, beating well after each addition. Blend in cocoa, flour and water. Beat well. Stir in pecans. In small mixing bowl, beat egg whites, cream of tartar and salt until stiff peaks form. Carefully fold into chocolate mixture. Pour into prepared pan. Bake 45 minutes or until top begins to crack slightly. (Cake will not test done in center.) Cool 1 hour. Cover and chill until firm. Remove side of pan. Pour Royal Glaze over cake, allowing glaze to run down side. Spread glaze evenly on top and side. Allow to set. Garnish with pecan halves, if desired. A total chocolate experience!!! Great dinner party dessert!

Yield: 10-12 servings

Evelyn Deane

Lemon Butter Tarts

6 whole eggs, beaten	3 dozen quarter sized tart shells
1 stick butter	from bakery
2 cups sugar	whipped cream
juice and rind of 2 lemons	

Chop butter into beaten eggs. Add sugar, juice and rind of lemons. Put in double boiler and stir constantly until spoon is coated thickly. Spoon into tarts and top with whipped cream. Will keep a couple weeks in refrigerator.

Yield: 3 dozen

Sissy Chesnutt

Meringue Shells

3 egg whites at room temperature	dash of salt
¼ teaspoon cream of tartar	1 cup sugar
1 teaspoon vanilla	

Combine egg whites, cream of tartar, vanilla and salt. Beat to soft peaks. Gradually add sugar, beat until stiff and glossy. Cover baking sheet with aluminum foil. Divide meringue into 8 mounds. Shape into shell with back of spoon. Bake at 275 for 2 hours. Turn off oven and keep oven door closed 1 hour or overnight. Serve with ice cream, sherbet or sorbet.

Yield: 8 servings

Kathy White

Hot Apple Spice Sundae

2 tablespoons butter or margurine	1 (21 ounce) can apple pie filling
2 tablespoons brown sugar	¼ cup chopped walnuts
½ teaspoon cinnamon	1 quart vanilla ice cream

Melt butter in saucepan. Stir in brown sugar, cinnamon and pie filling. Bring to a boil. Remove from heat and stir in walnuts. Serve warm over ice cream.

Yield: 6-8 servings

Diane With

217

Apple Crisp

½ cup white sugar
½ cup brown sugar
¾ cup flour
¼ cup margarine

4 cups apples, sliced thick
¼ cup water
1 tablespoon cinnamon

Work sugars, flour and butter together with fingers until crumbly. Place prepared apples in greased casserole dish. Pour water over apples and generously sprinkle with cinnamon. Spread crumb mixture over apples and bake uncovered at 350 for 50 minutes.

Yield: 8-10 servings

Sharon Hawkins

Fruit Cobbler

2 cans apple, peach or cherry pie filling
1 cup biscuit baking mix
¼ cup brown sugar

1 stick butter
cinnamon and sugar to taste
ice cream or whipped cream (optional)

Pour pie filling evenly in bottom of dish. Mix biscuit baking mix and brown sugar. Sprinkle evenly over fruit. Melt butter and pour over dry ingredients. Sprinkle with cinnamon and sugar. Bake at 350 for 45 minutes.

Yield: 10-12 servings

Lemon Dessert

1 small box lemon jello
2 cups water
1 cup sugar
1 can evaporated milk, chilled

juice of one lemon
rind of one lemon
mint sprig, optional

Prepare jello with 2 cups water. Add sugar and stir to dissolve. Let jello semi-set. Whip evaporated milk until soft peaks form. Fold into jello with lemon juice and rind. Pour into mold. Serve with a sprig of mint if desired.

Yield: 8-10 servings

Carol Kellum

Fruit Cobbler

1 cup sugar	½ cup butter or margarine
1 cup flour	1 giant can of fruit, drained or
1½ teaspoons baking powder	1 quart fresh fruit
¾ cup milk	sugar and cinnamon to taste

Mix sugar, flour, baking powder and milk together. Melt butter in a 9x13 inch baking dish. Add fruit to dish. Sprinkle top of fruit with sugar and cinnamon. Cover with flour mixture. Bake at 350 for 30-45 minutes or until browned and bubbly.

Yield: 10 servings

Leraine Collier

Fruit Cobbler

3 cups fresh fruit (apples, peaches, cherries or blueberries)	¾ cup self-rising flour
1 cup sugar	¾ cup sugar
1 teaspoon cinnamon (if you choose apples)	½ cup milk
	1 teaspoon vanilla
1 teaspoon nutmeg (if you choose peaches)	½ cup margarine

Cook the fruit and sugar in a small amount of water over low heat until the sugar dissolves. If you choose apples, add cinnamon. If you choose peaches, add nutmeg. Set aside. Stir together flour and sugar. Add milk and vanilla, mixing well. Melt margarine in 9x13 inch baking dish. Place fruit mixture in dish over butter. Spoon flour mixture over fruit. Bake at 375 for 30-40 minutes.

Yield: 8-10 servings

Linda Page

Pumpkin Crisp

1	can evaporated milk	1	box yellow cake mix
2	cans pumpkin	1	cup chopped nuts
1	cup sugar	2	sticks margarine, melted
2	eggs	1	teaspoon cinnamon

Icing:

8	ounces cream cheese, softened	1	small container frozen whipped
1½	cups powdered sugar		topping

Grease 9x13 inch pan. Mix milk, pumpkin, sugar, eggs and cinnamon. Spread in pan. Sprinkle with cake mix and pour margarine over this. Sprinkle with nuts. Bake at 325 for 60 minutes. Cool. Combine icing ingredients and spread over cooled cake.

Yield: 12 servings

Betty Lou Trimboli

Spiced Apple Charlotte

2	cups finely diced apples	½	cup orange juice
¾	cup sugar	3	tablespoons sherry
¼	teaspoon salt	¼	cup butter, melted
½	teaspoon ground cloves	3	cups soft bread crumbs
¼	teaspoon grated lemon rind		

Mix first seven ingredients. Combine butter and bread crumbs. Fill a buttered one quart casserole by layering crumbs and apples beginning and ending with crumbs. Cover and bake at 350 for 30 minutes. Uncover and bake 15 minutes longer. Serve warm.

Dina Trimboli Whitley, class of 80

Luscious Fruit Fluff

2	cups biscuit baking mix	1	teaspoon vanilla
2	tablespoons sugar	2	cups whipping cream
¼	cup butter	2	cups mini-marshmallows
6	ounces cream cheese, softened	4	cups mixed fresh fruit
1	cup sugar		

Mix first three ingredients until crumbly. Press into 9x9x2 inch ungreased pan. Bake at 375 for 15 minutes. Mix cheese, sugar and vanilla. Beat cream until stiff. Fold cream and marshmallows into mixture. Spread over crust. Chill at least eight hours. Serve with fresh fruit.

Dina Trimboli Whitley, class of 80

Fruit Pizza

1	(18 ounce) roll of refrigerator sugar cookie or 1 box sugar cookie mix		assorted fresh fruits (strawberries, blueberries, raspberries, cantaloupe, pineapple, kiwi,
1	(8 ounce) package cream cheese, regular, light or no-fat		bananas, etc.)
⅓	cup sugar	½	cup peach preserves (or strawberry)
½	teaspoon vanilla	2	tablespoons water

Spread cookie dough on 14 inch pizza pan. Bake at 375 for 10-12 minutes. Cool. Combine cream cheese, sugar and vanilla, mixing well. Spread over cooled crust. Arrange fruit in pleasing pattern on top. Mix preserves and water and glaze fruit. Chill. Serve in wedges like a pizza. Glaze may be omitted if desired.

Yield: 12 servings

Janet Carson Ricciarelli

Chocolate Sauce

1	stick butter, melted	½	cup white corn syrup
12	ounces chocolate chips		Kahlúa or vanilla
⅛	teaspoon salt	½	teaspoon cinnamon

Mix all ingredients except Kahlúa and cinnamon. Bring to a boil. Boil for two minutes over reduced heat. Add Kahlúa or vanilla to taste. Add cinnamon and stir. Serve warm over ice cream.

Yield: 6 servings

Creamy Cinnamon Spread

1	(8 ounce) package cream cheese, softened	1	teaspoon cinnamon
3	tablespoons powdered sugar	½	teaspoon vanilla extract

In a small bowl, beat all together using electric mixer until well blended. Store in an airtight container in refrigerator. Serve at room temperature.

Use your child's favorite cookie cutter to cut your morning toast. Top with Creamy Cinnamon Spread.

Carla Lancaster

Snow Cream

1	egg, beaten	2	tablespoons vanilla
¾	cup sugar	1	gallon snow
1	cup evaporated milk		

Combine egg and sugar. May omit egg. Mix in evaporated milk and vanilla. Add snow gradually.

Yield: 6 servings

Janet Carson Ricciarelli

Strawberry Bavarian Cream

1   (3 ounce) package strawberry
    flavored gelatin
2   cups hot water

1   cup heavy cream
2   cups strawberries, sliced

Combine gelatin and hot water according to package directions. Chill until syrup-like. Whip cream. Fold in whipped cream and strawberries to gelatin. Place in sherbet or parfait glasses.

Betty Lou Trimboli

Tropical Mousse

1   cup graham cracker crumbs
4   tablespoons butter, melted
2   tablespoons sugar
2   packages unfilled lady fingers
2   (8 ounce) packages cream
    cheese, softened
1   cup sifted powdered sugar
2   (1 pound, 4½ ounce) cans
    crushed pineapple, drained

2   (2 ounce) packages whipped
    topping mix
1   cup cold milk
1   teaspoon vanilla
frozen whipped topping for garnish
strawberries and pineapple rings for
    garnish

Combine graham crackers, butter and sugar. Press into bottom of a 9 inch springform pan. Line pan with ladyfingers, rounded side out. Whip cream cheese and powdered sugar until fluffy. Stir in crushed pineapple. Prepare both topping packages according to directions, using one cup of cold milk and one teaspoon of vanilla. Fold into pineapple mixture. Fill springform pan and chill at least six hours or overnight. When serving, this needs to be at room temperature 45-60 minutes to be sliced easily. After removing springform circle, garnish with frozen whipped topping, strawberries or pineapple rings.

Yield: 12 servings

Linda Haven

223

Forgotten Cookies

2-3 egg whites, beaten stiff with
    tartar
¼ teaspoon cream of tartar
⅔ cup sugar

1 teaspoon vanilla
1 cup mini chocolate chips
½ cup pecans (optional)

Preheat oven to 350. Drop dough by rounded teaspoons onto two large greased cookie sheets. Place in oven and immediately turn oven off. Leave cookies in oven overnight or until oven is cool.

Yield: 5 dozen

Joyce Gaudet Booth

Index

Making Time

The Arendell Parrott Academy Cookbook
P. O. Box 1297
Kinston, North Carolina 28503
(252) 522-4222

Please send me:

_____ copies of Making Time   at $18.95 each _____

Postage and handling   at $ 3.00 each _____

_____ copies of Frantic Elegance, the Arendell Parrott Academy
commemorative edition published in 1989, celebrating the twenty-
fifth anniversary of the Academy   at $13.50 each _____

Postage and handling   at $ 3.00 each _____

Name _____

Address _____

City _____ State _____ Zip _____

Make check payable to Arendell Parrott Academy.

-- --

Making Time

The Arendell Parrott Academy Cookbook
P. O. Box 1297
Kinston, North Carolina 28503
(252) 522-4222

Please send me:

_____ copies of Making Time   at $18.95 each _____

Postage and handling   at $ 3.00 each _____

_____ copies of Frantic Elegance, the Arendell Parrott Academy
commemorative edition published in 1989, celebrating the twenty-
fifth anniversary of the Academy   at $13.50 each _____

Postage and handling   at $ 3.00 each _____

Name _____

Address _____

City _____ State _____ Zip _____

Make check payable to Arendell Parrott Academy.

I would like to see *Making Time* in the following stores in my area:

Store Name _____

Address _____

City _____ State _____ Zip _____

Store Name _____

Address _____

City _____ State _____ Zip _____

- -

I would like to see *Making Time* in the following stores in my area:

Store Name _____

Address _____

City _____ State _____ Zip _____

Store Name _____

Address _____

City _____ State _____ Zip _____